SILENCING *the* NOISES WITHIN

How to Navigate Anxiety, Grief, and Depression
with Mindfulness and Resilience, Inspired by One
Man's Journey from Collapse to Clarity

A.W. HIYASAT

TABLE OF CONTENTS

.

ACKNOWLEDGMENTS

---

*I want to thank my family—especially **my wife**—for their unwavering encouragement throughout the journey of writing and publishing this book. Their support gave me the courage to share my story, a milestone I once doubted I could reach. In telling this story, I've learned to celebrate every accomplishment, big or small. And if this book speaks to and helps even one person, I will consider that a profound success.*

*I am deeply grateful to **my sister**, **Noor**, whose presence and encouragement helped bring this book to a higher level of meaning and purpose. Her thoughtful feedback, quiet strength, and belief in my message pushed me to dig deeper and stay true to the heart of this journey. Her support was a steady light during the most challenging moments, and I credit her with helping me shape this work into what it was truly meant to be.*

*I also extend my heartfelt thanks to **Hermione J. G**. for her steadfast partnership in bringing this dream to life. Her writing expertise and insight were invaluable throughout the process. I can honestly say that without her help, this book would not have reached the level of clarity, depth, and quality it now holds.*

INTRODUCTION

I couldn't speak.

The computer beeped, connecting me to yet another client. My mouth opened, but the words wouldn't come. Just silence. The script I'd repeated hundreds of times that day had vanished from my brain.

I grabbed my water bottle, took a quick sip, and tried again.

Nothing.

Then the tears came. Not a gentle misting of the eyes, but a flood I couldn't control. They spilled down my cheeks as I frantically waved my supervisor over, pointing at my stomach, faking some physical pain—anything but this humiliating emotional collapse.

I bolted from the building, head down, hoping no one would notice my tears. Once I was in my car, I fell apart completely. Sobbing so hard I couldn't see straight. Couldn't drive. Couldn't move. My body had made a decision my mind wasn't ready for: no more pretending. No more pushing through. No more "manning up."

Game over.

Looking back, it wasn't just anxiety or sadness that hit me that day. My entire system crashed after years of running on emotional fumes. I'd hit rock bottom. But in that terrible moment of breakdown, something unexpected happened.

The noise stopped.

For the first time in years, the constant chatter in my head went quiet. The endless loop of worries about my tanking career, the grief I'd stuffed down after my sister died, and the shame of ending up in a cubicle farm making cold calls after getting an MBA—it all just... stopped. Sitting there, crying like a lost child in my parked car, I felt a weird clarity: I couldn't keep living like this.

A few days later, I heard the words "severe depression and anxiety" from a doctor. And so began my long, messy crawl back from silence—the journey that changed everything. This book is about that crawl. About learning to speak again, in every sense of the word.

Before it all fell apart, I looked good on paper. MBA in hand, I'd jumped from a leadership role at a telecom company to what I thought would be a promising banking career. Had a wife. A son. A steady paycheck. The American dream, right?

But beneath that normal-looking life, everything was unraveling. The 2008 financial crisis hit just as I was trying to get my foot in the banking door. Leadership positions I interviewed for kept disappearing. Suddenly, I found myself in telemarketing—an MBA grad sitting shoulder-to-shoulder with kids barely out of high school, making cold calls to people who hated bankers with a passion.

And all this happened right after my sister died. She was just a year older than I was. Her death gouged a hole in my heart that I never properly dealt with. Instead, I did what men are taught to do—I buried that pain and kept moving. Because men don't cry. Men don't break down. Men provide. Men stay strong.

Men shut up and deal with it.

God, what a lie that is.

The perfect storm of career disaster, personal loss, and buried emotions slowly drowned me. But I didn't see it coming. Didn't recognize the warning signs. Didn't understand that a human mind, like any overloaded circuit, will eventually blow if the pressure keeps building.

Everyone around me saw a guy in a suit who had his act together. My family saw someone who kept pushing forward despite setbacks. But inside? I was drowning. And the gap between what people saw and what I felt just made things worse. How could I admit I wasn't coping when I had it better than so many others? How could I acknowledge weakness when I'd spent my whole life learning that real men push through pain?

That day in my car broke me open. It was the most humiliating moment of my life, but also the most necessary. Sometimes we need to hit the wall before we can change direction. My breakdown forced me to face truths I'd dodged for years.

Recovery was brutal. It took over a year of therapy sessions where I'd sit, sometimes still unable to speak, while tears ran down my face. Medication trials that made me twitch, rage, or sleep for 14 hours straight. I was slowly facing the mountain of anger and grief I'd been lugging around for years without even knowing it.

During this mess, I discovered I had ADHD—something that had made studying hell my entire life, but I'd just gritted my teeth and pushed through it. Amazing how much energy I'd wasted fighting my own brain instead of figuring out how it actually worked.

Healing didn't follow a nice, clean path. Some days I felt like myself again. Then came weeks where I could barely get out of bed. My marriage crumbled. I lost a business. For a while, I slept in my office because I had nowhere else to go. But something had fundamentally shifted in me. I wasn't running from my feelings anymore or pretending to be Superman. I was learning to face whatever came, messy as it was.

Brick by brick, I rebuilt. Earned a master's in accounting. Passed the CPA exam despite my ADHD making studying four times harder than it should've been. Started my own practice. Found unexpected joy in raising my kids and stepkids. Met someone who loved the real me, not the mask I'd worn for decades. Eventually, I even started a PhD, something I'd have laughed at during those dark days, crying in my car.

I'm telling this story because men are dying. Literally. We kill ourselves at rates three to four times higher than women (Centers for Disease Control and Prevention, 2025). Yet, we're the last to ask for help with depression, anxiety, or any other mental health issue. From boyhood, we learn that vulnerability means weakness, that emotional pain should be swallowed, and that needing help means you've failed as a man.

This silence is killing us.

I got lucky in a twisted way. My breakdown was so complete that I couldn't hide it anymore. It forced me to get help. But most guys suffer silently for years, their pain coming out sideways as rage, workaholism, drinking, or risky behavior. They—and often their families—never connect these dots to the deeper pain underneath.

Writing this book terrifies me. Laying bare my lowest moments feels like walking naked down Main Street. But if sharing my train wreck helps even one guy recognize himself in these pages, it's worth it. If you're reading this while your life is imploding—if you're barely hanging on while pretending everything's fine—know this: You are not alone. Asking for help isn't a weakness; it's the bravest damn thing you'll ever do.

This book shares the real strategies that pulled me back from the edge. Not polished, Instagram-worthy mental health tips, but the messy, imperfect tools that actually worked when nothing else did. Mindfulness practices that quieted the constant screaming in my head. Thought techniques that helped me stop the spiral of self-hatred. Simple daily habits that slowly rebuilt my broken foundation.

But more than anything, this book offers something I couldn't find in my darkest days: proof that rock bottom isn't the end of your story. It might actually be the beginning of a better one.

What makes this book different is that it's not written by some mental health guru who seems to have it all figured out since day one. It's written by a guy who completely fell apart and had to sweep up his own pieces. It acknowledges the specific barriers men face with mental health while giving you straightforward steps to clear those hurdles.

This book is for the guy lying awake at 3 a.m., mind racing with thoughts he can't control. For the man who feels increasingly numb and disconnected, wondering what happened to the person he used to be. It's also for those who love him—partners, family, and friends—who see him struggling but don't know how to help.

Throughout these pages, I'll show you how I escaped the overthinking trap that kept me locked in an endless loop of anxiety and depression. How I went from a man literally unable to speak to one who found his voice again—not just the physical ability to talk, but the deeper voice that comes from knowing who you are and what truly matters to you.

The moment when everything falls apart can be the exact moment a more honest life starts coming together.

My crash showed me that I'd been chasing all the wrong things—the promotion, the title, the external validation that never actually filled the hole inside me. In the silence that followed my breakdown, I started to hear what really mattered. I found out that happiness isn't in the BMW from the TV commercial or the "living my best life" vacation photos on Instagram. It's in knowing yourself, connecting with others, doing work that means something to you, and finding small moments of peace in a chaotic world.

If you're in that dark place now, where the noise in your head never stops and you're exhausted from pretending you're fine, I want you to know something: There comes a moment when that noise will stop. And in that silence, as terrifying as it feels at first, you might just find your way back to yourself.

This is the story of how I found mine.

Chapter 1:
The Unspoken Battle— Men, Depression, and the Path to Healing

---

> The most terrifying thing is to accept oneself completely.
>
> –Carl Jung

I didn't recognize depression when it came for me.

It didn't look like the commercials with the sad guy staring out rainy windows. It didn't match what I'd seen in movies or read about in magazines.

For me, depression wore the face of irritability. Of working 60-hour weeks. Of picking fights with my wife over nothing. Of drinking just enough to "take the edge off" most nights. The only tears came that final day in my car, after months—years, really—of feeling nothing but numb anger.

Nobody around me spotted it, either. Not my wife. Not my friends. Not even my doctor during my annual physical. Because men's depression often hides in plain sight, wearing disguises we don't recognize.

What's even more disturbing? That I'm not the exception; I'm the rule.

When we picture depression, we typically imagine someone who can't get out of bed, who cries frequently, and who withdraws from life. And yes, sometimes male depression looks exactly like that. But more often, it wears different masks—irritability, anger, recklessness, workaholism, and substance abuse. We don't call these depression. We call them "being an asshole" or "going through a rough patch" or, worst of all, "just being a guy."

Nobody taught me to recognize the warning signs in myself. Nobody said, "Hey, when men get depressed, they often get angry instead of sad." Nobody mentioned that emotional numbness—not feeling much of anything at all—can be a symptom, too. Or that constant overthinking, replaying conversations, and being unable to quiet your mind at night might be anxiety, not just "typical work stress."

We don't talk about how men's brains can betray us in unique ways. About how that voice in your head becomes increasingly critical, constantly replaying your failures while dismissing your successes. About how that overthinking trap keeps you spinning in circles until you're exhausted, but no closer to solutions.

For many of us, depression and anxiety don't announce themselves with convenient, obvious symptoms. They creep in slowly, disguising themselves as character flaws or normal responses to stress. *I'm not depressed*, we tell ourselves, *I'm just tired*. Or *I'm not anxious; I just care about doing a good job*. We dismiss the persistent insomnia, the racing thoughts, and the growing sense of disconnect from the people and activities we once enjoyed.

I've sat across from too many men in my therapy groups who said the same thing: "I had no idea this was depression. I thought I was just turning into an angry person." Or "I figured this was just what getting older felt like—being tired all the time and not looking forward to anything."

Make no mistake: This is a battle. It's a battle against outdated ideas about masculinity, against stigma, against a healthcare system that too often fails to recognize men's mental health issues until it's too late.

It's also a battle that, despite the grim statistics, can absolutely be won. I'm living proof of that. But first, we need to recognize the enemy for what it is, not what we've been told it should look like.

So, let's start by naming the unspoken battle that too many men are fighting alone. And then, let's talk about how to finally start winning it.

THE HIDDEN FACE OF MEN'S MENTAL HEALTH: BEHIND THE MASK

I bought a new suit for the interview. Dark blue, tailored to fit perfectly. The morning of, I got up early, shaved carefully, and even practiced my answers in the mirror. Walking into that bank for the leadership position, I looked every bit the successful MBA graduate ready for his next challenge. I had the firm handshake, the confident smile, and the polished answers.

No one would have guessed that just two nights before, I'd lain awake until 4 a.m., my thoughts racing so fast I couldn't catch them. No one would have known that on the drive there, I'd had to pull over because I couldn't catch my breath. And certainly no one would have suspected that behind my prepared answers about leadership philosophy and banking strategy, a voice in my head kept whispering, *Who are you kidding? You don't belong here.*

I got the news two weeks later. The position had been canceled due to the financial crisis. I nodded stoically on the phone, thanked them for the opportunity, and immediately applied for another opening. Externally, I was a resilience personified. Internally, I was crumbling.

Naming the unspoken battle that too many men are fighting alone

This was my life before the fall. A mask of competence covering a growing void. A daily performance of "having it together" while feeling increasingly hollow inside.

Looking back, the warning signs were everywhere. The insomnia. The irritability with my wife over trivial things. The way I'd snap at my son, then feel crushing guilt afterward. The increasing reliance on nighttime distractions—late-night TV, mindless scrolling, anything to avoid the stillness when the thoughts came rushing in. The growing sense that I was watching my life through a thick pane of glass, disconnected from everything around me.

But I didn't call it "depression." I called it "stress." I called it "a rough patch." I told myself all men feel this way sometimes.

I wasn't sad, and I wasn't crying. I was functioning. Therefore, I wasn't depressed.

This is the lie so many men tell themselves.

Here's what nobody told me until it was almost too late: Men's depression often wears a disguise. It doesn't always show up as the stereotypical sadness we see in TV commercials for antidepressants. For many of us, depression manifests as irritability, anger, recklessness, or a deep emotional numbness.

We look functional on the outside. We meet work deadlines. We show up at family dinners. We might even excel professionally while depression eats us from the inside out. We wear our suits like armor, masking the emptiness with achievement and stoicism.

I was that man. I was putting in long hours at the bank, volunteering for extra assignments, and doing everything possible to prove my worth after being demoted to telemarketing. My colleagues saw dedication. My family saw a provider determined to succeed. No one—including me—recognized it for what it really was: a desperate attempt to outrun the growing emptiness inside me.

This masking effect isn't unusual—it's the norm for men. We're taught from boyhood that our value lies in what we do, not how we feel. We learn that emotions are weaknesses to be conquered, not signals to be heeded. So, when depression creeps in, we don't reach for help. We reach for another project, another drink, another distraction.

The numbers tell the tragic story of where this leads. Women are diagnosed with depression roughly twice as often as men. Yet, men die by suicide at nearly four times the rate of women in most Western countries (Centers for Disease Control and Prevention, 2025). This isn't because women suffer more from depression; it's because men's depression remains invisible until it reaches catastrophic proportions.

Think about that gap. Really think about it. What's happening in that space between low diagnosis and high suicide rates? Men are suffering silently. Men are dismissing symptoms. Men are trying to power through unbearable pain because that's what men are taught to do.

I dismissed my symptoms for years. The sleepless nights? Just stress from work. The constant anxiety? Just being detail-oriented. The growing distance from my family and friends? Just being tired after long days.

Even physical symptoms didn't break through my denial. The racing heart. The constant headaches. The knot in my stomach that never went away. I popped antacids like candy and kept going.

My sister's death should have been my wake-up call. She was just a year older than I, closest in age and closest to me in spirit. We lived far apart as adults, but she remained my anchor, her calm voice grounding me whenever life felt overwhelming. When we were children, she was the one I turned to when I felt frustrated or angry. When I'd lash out over something like a toy my siblings wouldn't share, she'd gently say, "That one's not that fun—come play with this instead. I'll play with you." And just like that, the storm would pass.

When she died, I told myself I couldn't attend the funeral because of work. But that wasn't the real reason. The truth is that I couldn't face it. I didn't visit her grave until a year later, and only years after that did I realize I hadn't just been avoiding the trip—I was sidestepping my grief. Denial disguised as duty.

It wasn't until that day in my cubicle, when my voice literally failed me, that the mask finally cracked beyond repair.

If you're a man reading this, I want you to know something: Depression doesn't have to reach crisis point before you acknowledge it. You don't have to wait until you can't speak, or can't get out of bed, or can't see any way forward before you reach for help.

And if you're not experiencing depression but care about a man who might be, know that his suffering might not look like what you expect. Watch for the disguises:

- The guy who's suddenly working 70-hour weeks "because the project needs it"
- The friend who's drinking more but laughs it off as "just blowing off steam"
- The husband who seems perpetually irritated by small things that never bothered him before
- The father who's physically present but emotionally checked out
- The colleague whose risk-taking has suddenly increased

These might not look like depression to you—or to him—but they're often how men's depression first shows itself, hidden behind masks of masculinity we've been taught to wear.

I maintained my mask perfectly until it shattered completely. From the outside, I was still functioning right up until the moment I wasn't. I made my calls. I attended team meetings. I brought home paychecks. The gap between that external performance and my internal reality grew wider each day, until finally, it became an unbridgeable chasm.

The thing about masks is that they're exhausting to maintain. The energy it takes to appear fine when you're crumbling inside eventually depletes even the strongest among us. For me, that depletion happened in an instant—one moment I was speaking, the next I was mute, tears streaming down my face. For others, it might come as a heart attack triggered by unmanaged stress, an explosion of rage that destroys a relationship, or a night of drinking that ends in disaster.

But it doesn't have to reach that point. That's the message I wish someone had given me years earlier. You don't have to wait for complete collapse.

The statistics about men's suicide rates aren't just numbers to me. Each number represents a man who likely spent months or years hiding his suffering, believing he had to handle it alone, until the pain became so unbearable that ending his life seemed like the only escape. Each represents a mask worn too long, at too great a cost.

I was nearly one of those statistics. What saved me wasn't strength or resilience or any of those traits we're told make a man. What saved me was the complete failure of my ability to pretend anymore. My breaking point became my turning point.

But it doesn't have to reach a breaking point. We can learn to recognize depression's disguises earlier. We can understand that anger, numbness, and risk-taking might actually be depression wearing a mask. We can create space for men to seek help before a crisis hits.

The energy it takes to appear fine when you're crumbling inside eventually depletes even the strongest among us.

The overthinking trap—that constant spiral of negative thoughts—is particularly insidious for men. We don't call it "anxiety." We call it "problem-solving," "preparing," or "being responsible." But when your mind won't shut off at night, when you replay conversations searching for where you went wrong, when you constantly imagine worst-case scenarios—that's not just thinking. That's suffering.

Breaking free from that trap starts with recognition. With putting a name to what's happening in your mind. With understanding that what feels like "just how men think" might actually be depression or anxiety wearing one of its many disguises.

That recognition doesn't make you weak. It makes you self-aware. And self-awareness, not stoic suffering, is true strength.

UNDERSTANDING ANXIETY IN MEN: THE RESTLESS WARRIORS

I remember sitting in endless meetings at the bank, my leg bouncing under the table, a habit my colleagues found annoying. My stomach churned constantly, leading to a drawer full of antacids I'd pop throughout the day. At night, I'd lie awake, my heart racing while I mentally rehearsed the next day's calls, imagining every possible way they could go wrong.

Was I anxious? I would have laughed at the suggestion.

I was "prepared." I was "detail-oriented." I was "just a little stressed about hitting my numbers."

The word "anxiety" never entered my mind. That was something that happened to other people—probably people who couldn't handle pressure. And if there's one thing men are taught from boyhood, it's that we should be able to handle pressure.

It wasn't until years later, sitting across from a therapist who asked me to describe my physical symptoms, that I began to understand. What I'd been calling "work stress" was actually textbook anxiety. The racing heart, the churning stomach, the tension headaches, and the constant mental rehearsal of worst-case scenarios—all classic symptoms of an anxiety disorder that had been hiding in plain sight for years.

Men's anxiety wears camouflage. It disguises itself so well that we often don't recognize it in ourselves or in other men. We don't say, "I'm feeling anxious today." We say, "I'm stressed about this project," or "I can't seem to relax," or "I just need a drink to take the edge off."

And those around us—family, friends, even doctors—often miss it, too.

The physical symptoms of anxiety in men are deep but frequently mis-attributed. That knot in your stomach? It must be your diet. The tension headaches? Probably from staring at screens too long. The racing heart? Maybe you should cut back on caffeine. The constant fatigue? Everyone's tired these days.

We treat the symptoms while missing their source. I spent years taking antacids for stomach problems that were really anxiety. I tried sleeping pills for insomnia caused by racing thoughts. I blamed my irritability on other people's incompetence rather than recognizing it as my frayed nerves seeking an outlet.

Men develop creative ways to manage anxiety without ever calling it that. During my banking days, I'd work 14-hour days, telling myself I was "getting ahead" when, really, I was outrunning the thoughts that would catch up to me if I slowed down. After work, I'd hit the gym hard—not just for fitness, but because the physical exhaustion temporarily quieted my mind.

Some men manage anxiety through anger—the one emotion many of us feel comfortable expressing. That quick flare of temper over a small mistake might actually be anxiety in disguise. The road rage on your commute might be your body's way of channeling diffuse anxiety into something more familiar and acceptable for a man to feel.

Others seek relief through risk-taking behaviors—extreme sports, reckless driving, gambling, or casual sex. The adrenaline rush provides a temporary escape from the persistent low-level dread that anxiety creates. I knew guys at the bank who seemed addicted to closing high-risk deals—not just for the commission but for the temporary clarity that came with that risk-reward cycle.

What many men don't realize is how deeply anxiety affects our physical health. Our bodies aren't designed to sustain the stress response indefinitely. The constantly elevated cortisol, the perpetually tensed muscles, and the disrupted sleep take a serious toll over time.

I learned this the hard way. After years of untreated anxiety, my body started sending louder signals I couldn't ignore. My blood pressure climbed into dangerous territory. I developed persistent digestive issues that no medication seemed to touch. My immune system weakened, leaving me vulnerable to catching every cold that circulated through the office.

And then came the panic attacks—though I didn't call them that at the time. I called them "episodes" or "weird spells." They'd hit without warning. My heart would race, my vision would narrow, and I'd be convinced I was having a heart attack. The first time it happened, I ended up in the emergency room, hooked to monitors while doctors found nothing physically wrong with me.

"It's probably just stress," they said, prescribing nothing more than "try to relax."

As if I hadn't been trying to do exactly that for years.

This is a common experience for men with anxiety. We enter the health-care system complaining of physical symptoms—heart palpitations, chest pain, digestive issues, sexual dysfunction, or unexplained pain. We get tests. The tests come back normal. We're told it's "just stress" and sent on our way without real treatment for the underlying anxiety disorder slowly damaging our health.

Untreated anxiety significantly increases your risk for serious health problems. Your risk of heart disease climbs. Your chance of developing a substance use disorder skyrockets. Your immune system weakens. Even your digestive system and sexual function suffer.

Anxiety isn't "just in your head." It's in your entire body.

I think of men with anxiety as restless warriors. We're fighting battles on multiple fronts—against the external pressures of work and life, against our bodies' alarm systems that won't stop ringing, and against the cultural expectations that tell us we shouldn't be struggling in the first place.

It's exhausting. And, unlike external enemies, anxiety can't be defeated through sheer force of will or working harder.

If you're reading this and recognizing yourself or someone you care about, know that anxiety doesn't have to be a life sentence. Men can learn to recognize anxiety for what it is, to name it accurately rather than calling it stress or pressure. We can develop healthier strategies for managing it than overworking, substance use, or anger.

Most importantly, we can break the overthinking cycle that keeps anxiety fed and flourishing.

Men with anxiety aren't weak. We're often the ones pushing hardest, achieving the most, and appearing the strongest to the outside world. We're warriors fighting invisible battles others can't see. But every warrior needs rest, strategy, and the right weapons for the fight ahead.

Anxiety isn't "just in your head."
It's in your entire body

BREAKING THE SILENCE: WHY MEN DON'T REACH OUT

I sat in my parked car, tears streaming down my face, unable to drive, unable to speak, unable even to think clearly. Yet, in that moment of complete breakdown, a thought still managed to push through: *Nobody can see me like this.*

Not my wife. Not my friends. Not my coworkers. Nobody.

Even at my absolute lowest point—literally unable to form words—my instinct was to hide. I flagged my supervisor over, pointed at my stomach, and pretended I had physical pain rather than admit I was crying. I rushed out of the building with my head down, desperate to hide my tears.

Why? Why was appearing strong more important than getting help? Why was I more afraid of someone seeing me cry than of the terrifying mental collapse I was experiencing?

The answer lies in lessons I'd been absorbing since before I could form complete sentences.

When I was five, I fell off my bike and scraped my knee badly. I remember my father helping me up, dusting me off, and saying with affection but firmness, "You're okay. Big boys don't cry." He wasn't being cruel; he was teaching me what he'd been taught and preparing me for a world he understood.

By the time I was seven, I'd already learned that emotions had no place in a boy's toolkit. When I came down with a contagious illness that left me bedridden for over a month, I was kept isolated from my siblings. No visits. Just notebooks, pens, and a stack of comic books. I was fatigued, frustrated, and desperate to go outside and play. But I didn't complain—I understood that being upset wasn't an option. Even at that age, I had absorbed the message: Young men endure, and they endure quietly.

By the time I reached adulthood, the walls around my emotions were fortress-thick. I could feel anger—that was acceptable. I could feel pride—that was encouraged. But sadness, fear, uncertainty, vulnerability? Those had no place in my emotional vocabulary.

This isn't just my story. It's the story of most men in our society.

From our earliest days, we're taught to suppress emotional vulnerability: "Man up." "Don't be a sissy." "Rub some dirt on it." These seemingly harmless phrases carry a powerful subtext: Your feelings don't matter, your pain isn't important, and showing either makes you less of a man.

We learn these lessons everywhere—from fathers and coaches, from books and movies, from watching how other boys who show emotion are treated. By adulthood, most men have developed such a deep disconnect from their emotional lives that they literally cannot identify what they're feeling beyond basic categories such as "pissed off" or "fine."

I couldn't. For years, if you'd asked me how I was feeling, I'd have said "stressed" or "tired" or "fine"—never "sad" or "scared" or "overwhelmed." Those words weren't in my emotional vocabulary. They felt feminine, weak, and inappropriate for a man to express.

Even when depression hit me hard after my sister's death, I didn't see it as a legitimate health condition. I saw it as a character flaw, a weakness I needed to overcome through willpower and hard work. When anxiety kept me awake night after night, I didn't think, *I should talk to someone about this*. I thought, *I need to get tougher*.

The cultural stories around masculinity made this disconnect even deeper. Think about the male heroes we grew up watching. John Wayne never cried. James Bond never sought therapy. Batman didn't process his grief—he channeled it into punching criminals. Our cultural icons solve problems alone, endure suffering silently, and emerge stronger through solitary struggle.

Yes, these stories are for entertainment, but they've become blueprints for how we believe men should behave. They've taught us that real men handle their problems alone. That asking for help is a last resort, an admission of failure. That silence equals strength.

I believed those stories completely. I also saw what happened to men who didn't. In high school, I watched a teammate break down crying after a tough loss. The merciless teasing that followed lasted weeks. In college, a friend admitted to feeling depressed after a breakup and was mockingly called "emo" behind his back.

The message was clear: If you display vulnerability, you'll suffer the consequences.

By the time I was in my thirties, working at the bank and spiraling into depression, the walls around my emotions were impenetrable. I'd witnessed and internalized the social penalties for male vulnerability. I'd seen the ridicule, the diminished respect, and the questioning of masculinity that followed any display of emotional struggle.

Why would I risk that? Why would any man?

These psychological barriers were powerful enough, but practical obstacles made seeking help even more difficult. As my family's primary provider, I viewed any time spent on my mental health as selfish or unnecessary. There were bills to pay, deadlines to meet, and responsibilities to fulfill. Taking an afternoon off for therapy? That seemed like an indulgence I couldn't afford.

The nature of therapy itself presented another barrier. As men, we're action-oriented problem-solvers. We want to fix things, preferably quickly and efficiently. But therapy doesn't work that way. It's reflective, process-oriented, sometimes slow, and rarely linear. It asks you to sit with your feelings rather than immediately trying to fix them—the exact opposite of how most men approach problems.

Even scheduling was a hurdle. Like many men, I prioritized work commitments over healthcare appointments. I'd reschedule my annual physical three times to accommodate client meetings, but wouldn't dream of asking a client to reschedule for me. My health—especially my mental health—always came last.

All these barriers—societal expectations, cultural narratives, practical obstacles—form a perfect storm that keeps men from reaching out until crisis hits. Often, not even then.

I was "lucky" in a twisted way. My breakdown was so complete, so physically overwhelming, that it finally broke through my resistance. When you can't speak, can't stop crying, and can't function at the most basic level, it becomes impossible to maintain the fiction that you're fine. My body made the decision my mind had refused to make.

But what about the millions of men suffering silently who never reach that breaking point? Men who manage to maintain their masks, even as depression or anxiety hollows them out from the inside? Men who keep pushing forward, believing they can outwork or outwill their mental health challenges?

Many never get help at all. Others reach for unhealthy substitutes—drugs, risk-taking behaviors, anger, and so on—that temporarily mask the pain without addressing its source. Some hold on until physical symptoms force them into the healthcare system for issues seemingly unrelated to mental health—heart problems, chronic pain, digestive issues, and sexual dysfunction, among others.

And too many become statistics in our suicide rates, having never spoken about their suffering to anyone.

If you're reading this and recognize yourself in these words, know that you don't have to wait for a complete breakdown to seek help. The walls that keep you silent aren't protecting you; they're isolating you. And you're not alone in struggling to break them down.

RECOGNIZING DEPRESSION'S SIGNALS IN YOURSELF AND OTHERS

"How are you doing?"

It's such a simple question. So, why did it leave me staring blankly at my friend across the lunch table? He'd noticed I hadn't been myself lately and decided to check in. A normal human would have an answer ready. I didn't.

"I'm fine," I finally said. The universal response. The safe response.

But I wasn't fine. I just didn't have the words to describe what was happening inside me. I wasn't sad, exactly. I wasn't crying all the time or unable to get out of bed—the behaviors I associated with depression. I was just... empty. Going through the motions. Working, eating, sleeping, repeating. My life had become mechanical, like I was watching someone else live it through a thick pane of glass.

If my friend had asked, "Are you depressed?" I would have immediately said no. Depression meant sadness, and I wasn't sad. I was irritable. Restless. Emotionally flat. Increasingly reliant on distractions to quiet my mind at night. Working longer hours to avoid going home to a family I couldn't emotionally connect with.

Depression in men often wears a disguise. It hides behind the mask of functionality—what doctors sometimes call "masked depression" or "male-type depression" (Fulmali et al., 2018). While we picture depression as persistent sadness and crying, for many men, it shows up differently.

Instead of tears, there's irritability. Instead of expressing sadness, there's emotional numbness. Instead of talking about feeling worthless, there's hypersensitivity to criticism. Instead of saying "I'm depressed," there's "I'm stressed," "I'm fine," or "Just tired."

Men's depression often goes undiagnosed because we're looking for the wrong signs.

Think about how depression is typically portrayed: a person crying, staying in bed, and explicitly expressing sadness or worthlessness. That's certainly how depression manifests for many people. But for many men, the experience is fundamentally different.

When depression hit me, I didn't feel persistently sad. I felt empty. Flat. I described it to my therapist later as "feeling like a robot." I went through the required motions of life without actually experiencing engagement or meaning. Work, which I'd once found challenging and rewarding, became merely something I did to pay bills. Time with my family, which should have brought me joy, felt like another performance I had to get through.

This difference in how depression presents in many men contributes significantly to underdiagnosis. Standard depression screenings ask about sadness, crying, and feelings of worthlessness—symptoms many depressed men don't consistently experience. Public awareness campaigns show images that don't match how many men experience depression. So, both the men themselves and those around them miss the warning signs until the situation becomes critical.

Perhaps most telling are the behavioral changes that often accompany male depression. Rather than directly expressing emotional pain, many men turn to escapism or self-medication.

Other common behavioral changes include increased substance use, compulsive sexual behavior, excessive gaming, risk-taking behaviors, and gambling. Like drinking and overworking, these behaviors often intensify over time as tolerance develops. They create additional problems while masking the underlying depression—a dangerous cycle that can continue for years.

Physical symptoms provided more clues that I missed. My sleep became increasingly disrupted—I'd lie awake for hours with racing thoughts, then feel exhausted all day. My energy plummeted. I developed persistent headaches and back pain that no amount of ibuprofen seemed to touch. My appetite changed—sometimes I wasn't hungry for days; other times I ate constantly without really tasting the food. My sex drive virtually disappeared.

I attributed all these to aging, stress, or too much screen time, never considering they might have psychological origins. Again, this is typical. Men often view physical symptoms through a purely physical lens, missing their connection to mental health.

Early recognition is crucial because untreated depression typically worsens over time and significantly increases suicide risk. The longer depression goes untreated, the more deeply entrenched it becomes and the more it affects every aspect of life—work, relationships, and physical health.

For those concerned about a man in their life, certain conversational shifts can indicate depression. Listen for increased negativity or cynicism from someone previously optimistic. Notice when a man who used to share thoughts and feelings becomes increasingly closed or responds to questions about his well-being with brief, dismissive answers. Pay attention when someone who used to have goals and plans for the future stops mentioning them, focusing solely on getting through the present day.

The language men use to describe their experience often provides clues, as well. While women more frequently use emotional language like "sad" or "depressed," men might say:

- "I feel nothing."
- "I'm just going through the motions."

- "Everything feels like a struggle."

- "I can't seem to focus on anything."

- "I don't see the point anymore."

- "I'm always on edge lately."

These expressions reflect the emptiness, mechanical functioning, and irritability that often characterize male depression.

Sleep changes offer another window into potential depression. Does he have trouble falling asleep despite being exhausted? Does he wake up at 3 a.m. with racing thoughts? Does he sleep excessively on weekends, trying to "catch up" but never feeling rested? All might indicate the sleep disruption common in depression.

Risk-taking behavior sometimes increases, as well—driving too fast, gambling larger amounts, seeking out casual sexual encounters, taking physical risks that seem out of character. For some depressed men, the adrenaline rush of risk temporarily breaks through the emotional numbness, becoming addictive in its own right.

WHEN EVERYTHING CRUMBLES: FINDING GROUND IN THE LANDSLIDE

I remember exactly where I was sitting when they told me my position had been eliminated—a beige conference room with those generic motivational posters about "teamwork" and "excellence." The irony wasn't lost on me. I nodded professionally as HR explained my severance package. We shook hands. I cleaned out my desk. I drove home. All without showing a crack in my composure.

Three months earlier, my sister had died unexpectedly at 36. One month before that, the 2008 financial crisis had hit, evaporating a significant chunk of our savings practically overnight. Now, my leadership position was gone, too, restructured out of existence as the bank scrambled to survive the economic meltdown.

It wasn't just one thing going wrong. It was everything, all at once.

I walked into my house that evening, set my box of desk items on the kitchen counter, and told my wife the news with the same flat affect I'd maintained all day. She hugged me. She cried a little. I didn't. I told her we'd be okay, that I'd start looking for a new position immediately, and that my network was strong.

I believed none of it. But admitting that felt impossible.

That night, lying awake at 3 a.m. while my wife slept beside me, I felt something break loose inside me—not tears or grief or even fear, but a deep disorientation. Who was I now? The steady career trajectory that had defined my adult identity had vanished. The financial security I'd prided myself on providing for my family was suddenly precarious. She wasn't my only sister, but she was the one I shared the deepest bond with—closest in age and closest to my heart. My childhood ally, my emotional anchor. Losing her felt like losing a part of myself.

Every pillar I'd built my identity around was crumbling simultaneously.

This wasn't just sadness or disappointment. It was an earthquake beneath the very foundation of my life. Everything I thought I knew about myself, my future, and how the world worked had been upended all at once.

When multiple crises hit simultaneously—financial collapse, career loss, death of loved ones—the impact isn't simply additive. It's exponential. One crisis depletes your emotional reserves. The second crisis hits those already-depleted resources. By the third, you're running on fumes, with no recovery period between blows.

I'd always considered myself resilient. I'd faced setbacks before and pushed through them. But this perfect storm was different. It wasn't just about enduring temporary pain; it was about losing the very coordinates I'd always navigated my life by.

For men, especially, simultaneous professional and personal crises create a particularly devastating challenge to identity. Whether we admit it or not, traditional masculine identity remains heavily tied to professional achievement and provider status. I'd never considered myself particularly traditional in my views, but losing my career and financial stability hit me at a core level I hadn't fully recognized until they were gone.

What was I worth now? Who was I if not a successful banking executive? How could I face my son if I couldn't provide the life I'd promised him? These questions plagued me during those sleepless nights, creating a spiral of doubt that undermined any confidence I had left.

The grief over my sister became tangled up in these other losses. I'd push thoughts of her away because I "needed to focus on finding work." I'd feel guilty about worrying about money when she had lost her very life. The natural progression through grief that might have happened if that were my only loss became impossible as multiple traumas competed for my limited emotional bandwidth.

I didn't have words for what I was experiencing then. Now, I understand it was an existential crisis—a deep questioning of my worth, purpose, and very sense of self. Without the external markers of value and meaning I'd relied on, I felt untethered, adrift in a world suddenly revealed as chaotic and unpredictable.

This wasn't ordinary sadness or even typical grief. It was a fundamental disruption of the narratives through which I understood myself and my place in the world. The story I'd been telling myself about who I was and where my life was heading had been shattered beyond recognition.

Looking back, I see how unprepared I was for this kind of multilayered collapse. Our culture provides some frameworks for handling single losses—there are books about grief after losing a loved one, support groups for job loss, and financial advisors for economic hardship. But when everything crumbles at once? The resources are scarce.

This gap left me without adequate frameworks for processing my experiences. And like most men facing a financial crisis, practical survival concerns took immediate precedence over emotional processing. I needed to find work. I needed to figure out our budget. I needed to keep the lights on and food on the table.

So, I did what seemed logical: I pushed the emotions aside and focused on practical solutions. I updated my résumé. I called contacts. I took the first position offered—a significant step down from my previous role, but a paycheck nonetheless. I cut our expenses to the bone. I put one foot in front of the other and kept moving.

What I didn't realize was that emotions don't simply disappear when ignored. They go underground, gathering force like water behind a dam. My unprocessed grief, fear, and shame didn't evaporate because I was too busy to deal with them. They seeped into every aspect of my life, emerging as irritability, insomnia, and eventually, the complete breakdown in my cubicle years later.

That breakdown—the moment when my voice literally failed me and I couldn't stop crying—wasn't just about the telemarketing job I hated. It was the delayed reaction to losses I'd never properly faced. It was years of unprocessed grief finally breaching the emotional dam I'd built to hold it back.

When that dam broke, the noise in my head finally stopped. The constant anxiety, the endless mental rehearsal of worst-case scenarios, and the perpetual strategizing about how to fix my broken life—it all went silent in that moment of complete surrender. I couldn't think myself out of this. I couldn't work harder or push through or maintain the façade of control any longer.

Emotions don't simply disappear when ignored. They go underground, gathering force like water behind a dam

Everything had crumbled, including my ability to pretend otherwise.

That terrifying silence turned out to be the beginning of actual healing. Not the band-aid solutions I'd been applying to gaping wounds, but genuine recognition of how deeply I'd been affected by these concurrent losses. It was the first honest moment I'd had with myself in years.

If you're in that landslide right now—if multiple crises have hit you simultaneously and you feel like you're losing your grip on everything familiar—know that you're facing something extraordinarily difficult, even if you're trying to convince yourself and everyone else that you're fine.

The confusion, disorientation, and identity disruption you might be experiencing aren't signs of weakness or failure. They're normal responses to abnormal circumstances. When multiple foundational aspects of your life crumble simultaneously, disorientation isn't just common—it's practically inevitable.

But here's what I learned the hard way: Pretending you're on solid ground when you're actually in a landslide doesn't make you strong. It just ensures you'll keep getting buried deeper.

Finding actual ground in the landslide requires first acknowledging that the landscape has changed. What you're experiencing isn't business as usual. Those concurrent crises create psychological impacts greater than the sum of their parts.

It means allowing yourself to feel disoriented without immediately trying to force certainty where none exists. It means recognizing that your identity is undergoing a huge shift—not because you've failed, but because the external markers you built that identity around have changed or disappeared.

Most of all, it means understanding that dealing with multiple simultaneous losses requires different strategies than handling isolated challenges.

You can't just "push through" or "stay busy" until things get better. The emotional weight is too great, the identity disruption too immense.

If you're in the landslide now, know that while I can't promise when or how your particular path will stabilize, I can tell you with certainty that solid ground does exist. Not where it used to be, and not looking like what you expected, but it's there, and finding it might lead you to building something stronger than what was lost.

CHAPTER 2:
FROM DARKNESS TO STRENGTH— REDISCOVERING YOUR POWER THROUGH VULNERABILITY

The wound is the place where the Light enters you.

–RUMI

I sat in my therapist's office, staring at the floor. "I don't know how to do this," I admitted.

"Do what, exactly?" she asked.

"Be weak." The words felt like gravel in my mouth.

She leaned forward slightly. "Is that what you think this is? Weakness?"

I looked up, confused. "What else would you call it? I broke down crying at work. I can't sleep. I can't stop my thoughts from spiraling. I'm sitting here talking about my feelings. If that's not weakness, what is it?"

Her answer changed everything: "I'd call it courage."

That conversation marked the beginning of my journey toward understanding true strength—not as the absence of struggle, but as the willingness to face it honestly. Not as emotional invulnerability, but as emotional authenticity. Not as having all the answers, but as being brave enough to ask for help.

THE ARMOR WE CARRY:
UNDERSTANDING MASCULINE EXPECTATIONS

We don't tend to think about the psychological weight of being a man in today's world. But make no mistake—it's heavy. The modern male experience involves negotiating a maze of contradictory expectations that would make anyone's head spin.

- Be strong but vulnerable (but not too vulnerable).
- Be confident, but never arrogant.
- Be successful, but don't focus too much on material things.
- Be emotionally available, but never weak.
- Be masculine, but reject toxic masculinity.

These aren't just minor mixed signals. They're fundamentally contradictory demands that create what psychologists call "masculine gender role stress," a fancy term for the chronic strain that comes from trying to fulfill mutually exclusive ideals (Aguilera et al., 2024).

I felt this strain acutely throughout my corporate career. In leadership meetings, I needed to project unflappable confidence and decisiveness. With my team, I was expected to show empathy and emotional intelligence. At home, I was supposed to leave work stress at the door and be fully present. With friends, I needed to be relaxed and authentic. With my son, I needed to model both traditional strength and modern emotional openness.

The armor kept getting heavier, with new pieces added for each environment, until I was barely able to move under the weight.

For many men, this unwinnable situation creates a persistent sense of inadequacy and fraudulence. We never feel we've achieved "true" masculinity because it's impossible to simultaneously fulfill all the contradictory expectations placed upon us. We're always failing at some aspect of manhood, no matter how hard we try.

This psychological burden creates fertile ground for depression and anxiety, especially when combined with the emotional restraint most men are conditioned to maintain from childhood. We're trained to limit our emotional expression to a narrow range—pride, determination, controlled anger in appropriate contexts—while suppressing vulnerability, fear, confusion, or hurt.

I became so good at this suppression that I lost awareness of my emotions entirely. During my banking years, colleagues commented on my indefatigable demeanor during crises. What looked like admirable composure was actually emotional numbness. I wasn't staying calm; I simply couldn't access my feelings in the moment. They would emerge later as insomnia, tension headaches, or irritability at home, disconnected from their source.

The psychological cost of this chronic emotional suppression goes far beyond momentary discomfort. Consistently inhibiting emotional expression requires significant cognitive resources. It's like running background processes on your computer that drain processing power and battery life. Your mind is constantly monitoring, suppressing, and controlling emotions, leaving fewer mental resources for everything else in your life.

Over time, this suppression correlates with increased inflammation in the body, hormonal imbalances, and changes in brain activity associated with depression. Your body literally pays the price for emotions your mind refuses to process.

Many men describe feeling "emotionally color-blind," able to recognize only a narrow band of acceptable feelings while more nuanced emotions remain unavailable to conscious awareness. I couldn't tell you whether I felt disappointed, lonely, or anxious—it was all just "stress" to me. This emotional constriction limits access to the full spectrum of human experience and creates deep loneliness, as we cannot share what we cannot name or recognize within ourselves.

The current crisis of masculinity stems partly from rapid social change that has altered traditional male roles without providing clear alternatives. The economic landscape has shifted dramatically, disrupting men's historical notion that they are the sole providers. Manufacturing jobs that once offered stable middle-class livelihoods have disappeared. Education systems seem increasingly designed for learning styles that don't favor many boys. Evolving gender norms have questioned many traditional masculine behaviors without offering coherent new ideals.

This ambiguity leaves many men caught between outdated models we recognize as problematic and a vacuum of clear, positive masculine identity. We know the old armor is too rigid, too heavy, and too limiting—but we're not sure what to replace it with.

I see this confusion in men across generations. Older men who play by rules that no longer apply. Middle-aged men like myself, caught in the transition, trying to retain what was valuable from traditional masculinity while adapting to new expectations. Younger men are inheriting an environment of masculine identity that's more uncertain than ever.

This uncertainty breeds overthinking. Without clear guidelines, we constantly second-guess ourselves. *Is this response too aggressive? Not assertive enough? Am I being emotionally authentic or indulgently weak? Should I speak up or listen? Take charge or collaborate?* The mental calculations never stop.

DEPRESSION'S DIFFERENT FACE: HOW MEN EXPERIENCE THE DARKNESS

"Why are you always so angry lately?"

My wife's question stopped me in my tracks. I wasn't angry. I was just... I didn't know what I was. Tired. Stressed. Overwhelmed by the constant noise in my head. But angry? I didn't feel angry.

"I'm not angry," I snapped back. "I'm just trying to get things done around here without everyone constantly needing something from me."

I heard the edge in my voice even as I denied its existence. The look on her face told me everything I needed to know—this wasn't the first time we'd had this conversation. I was irritable all the time, quick to flare up over minor inconveniences, sarcastic where I used to be playful, and critical where I used to be supportive.

I didn't recognize this version of myself, but everyone around me did. They were walking on eggshells, carefully monitoring their words and needs to avoid setting me off. And I was completely blind to it.

This is one of depression's cruelest tricks in men; it often doesn't feel like sadness at all. It feels like irritation. Frustration. Cynicism. A short fuse where there used to be patience.

There's an old expression that "depression is anger turned inward," but for many men, it works in reverse; depression turns outward as irritability, hostility, or even explosive anger. These externalizing symptoms reflect both biological factors and the way we're raised. We're taught from childhood that anger is an acceptable male emotion, while vulnerability is discouraged. So, when depression hits, it often speaks through the emotional language we've been allowed to develop.

For me, and for many men, escalating irritability represents the most noticeable shift during depression's onset. Our families often spot this change long before we recognize anything amiss. My wife saw my depression taking hold months before I had any clue what was happening to me.

This anger-depression connection creates particular challenges in relationships. When someone is sad, our natural response is compassion. But when someone is hostile or irritable, our instinct is to become defensive or withdraw. We respond to anger with distance rather than support, which means that depressed men often find themselves increasingly isolated exactly when they most need connection.

Another way depression often shows its face in men is through self-medication and risk-taking. When the emotional numbness of depression sets in—that deadened feeling where nothing brings joy or interest—many men instinctively reach for something that can break through the numbness, even temporarily.

Risk-taking often increases during depressive episodes, too. Dangerous driving, extreme sports without proper safety measures, physical confrontations, and financial gambles—these behaviors serve both as escape and as physical manifestations of self-destructive urges. The adrenaline rush temporarily breaks through depression's emotional flatness, creating a false but addictive sense of feeling alive.

I found myself driving faster than usual during my darkest period, taking corners too quickly, pushing the limits in ways that weren't obvious suicide attempts but weren't entirely about survival, either. The momentary rush of fear helped me feel something, anything, beyond the pervasive emptiness.

These behaviors create a dangerous cycle. Their consequences—legal problems, relationship damage, financial strain—typically worsen the underlying depression, leading to more self-destructive behavior and creating more negative consequences. The spiral pulls you deeper with each rotation.

Depression's physical symptoms in men also deserve attention. Beyond the commonly recognized sleep and appetite changes, many men experience persistent pain conditions, digestive troubles, and sexual dysfunction during depression. Headaches that don't respond to pain relievers. Back pain with no clear physical cause. Stomach issues that doctors can't quite diagnose.

These aren't "just in your head"; they're real physical manifestations of depression's impact on your body.

Understanding these different faces of depression in men isn't just academic; it can truly save lives. When we recognize that depression might look like anger rather than sadness, like risk-taking rather than withdrawal, like physical complaints rather than expressed hopelessness, we open the door to earlier intervention.

It doesn't have to take long. Learning to recognize depression's different faces in men—in yourself or someone you care about—can lead to support and treatment before the darkness becomes overwhelming. The noise in your head, the irritability that pushes others away, the behaviors that temporarily distract but ultimately harm—they're not who you are. They're symptoms of a treatable condition that millions of men experience.

The first step toward quieting that noise is recognizing where it's coming from.

TAKING OFF THE MASK:
FINDING STRENGTH IN AUTHENTICITY

The most terrifying moment of my life wasn't when I broke down crying in my cubicle. It was the day after, when I had to decide whether to return to work wearing my usual mask or to finally let someone see the truth.

The first step toward quieting that noise
is recognizing where it's coming from

For weeks after my sister's funeral, I'd been struggling to speak at all. Words would form in my mind but die before reaching my lips. My voice would simply disappear mid-sentence, as if someone had cut the connection between my brain and my mouth. My doctor called it "situational mutism"—a rare response to extreme stress or trauma.

Yet, I'd kept showing up to work each day, pretending everything was fine. I'd nod in meetings, send emails, and when absolutely necessary, force out brief responses in a voice that didn't sound like my own. I was dying inside while maintaining a perfect façade of normalcy.

Until that day in the cubicle when the mask finally shattered completely.

After calling in sick and spending a sleepless night staring at the ceiling, I faced a choice: continue the exhausting performance that was breaking me, or do something that felt far more dangerous—tell the truth.

My wife had to call my supervisor to let him know I wouldn't be coming to work for several days. She told him I was ill, but she didn't give any specifics—mostly because there weren't any that made sense yet. Eventually, my supervisor asked me to speak with him directly.

I sat beside my wife as she held the phone and called him. He answered with a casual greeting. I tried to respond, but nothing came out. Just noise. Panic surged through me. I reached for a notepad and scribbled a message to my wife: "Can you talk to him? Tell him I'm here, but I can't speak." She nodded and began explaining what I couldn't. And in that moment, against every instinct I had, I let her. Every fiber of my being screamed that I was violating the code—the man code—by showing weakness, by admitting I was vulnerable and not in control. But I was already past the point of pretending.

But here's what happened: nothing terrible. My supervisor didn't mock me or think less of me. He didn't question my competence or manhood. He simply said, "I'm glad you told me. What do you need?"

That moment marked the beginning of my seeking a different kind of strength, not the false strength of pretending to be invincible, but the genuine strength of authenticity.

Embracing this new kind of courage represents a critical step in men's recovery from depression. It requires challenging the beliefs about masculinity we've carried since childhood, beliefs so deeply internalized they feel like absolute truths rather than cultural constructs.

For me, those beliefs included:

- Real men handle problems alone.

- Showing emotion equals weakness.

- Needing help means you're inadequate.

- Control must be maintained at all costs.

These weren't ideas I consciously chose; they were messages absorbed from every direction since I was old enough to understand what being a "good man" meant. From my father's stoic response to adversity. From coaches who taught us to "walk it off" when injured. From movies where male heroes suffer in silence. From watching other boys get ridiculed for crying.

Challenging these beliefs felt like questioning gravity. But, as it turned out, that's exactly what recovery required.

I had to expand my definition of strength beyond stoic silence to include the courage to acknowledge vulnerability, to stand authentically in the full spectrum of human experience rather than limiting myself to culturally approved emotions. This expanded definition recognized that facing emotions requires greater courage than avoiding them. Seeking appropriate help demonstrates greater wisdom than suffering in isolation. That genuine inner strength emerges from emotional flexibility rather than rigid control.

This redefinition process began with recognizing how traditional masculine ideals had limited rather than enhanced my life and relationships. My commitment to handling everything alone had left me isolated in my suffering. My suppression of "unacceptable" emotions had disconnected me from myself and others. My refusal to seek help had prolonged my depression far beyond what was necessary.

The mask I thought was protecting me was actually suffocating me.

To be honest, removing that mask required developing skills I'd never been taught, starting with basic emotional literacy. I entered therapy as an emotional novice, having spent decades disconnected from my inner world. I couldn't identify or name what I was feeling beyond basic categories like "stressed," "fine," or occasionally "angry."

My therapist gave me practical approaches that felt awkward at first, but they gradually built my emotional vocabulary. Regular emotional check-ins became part of my daily routine; I paused several times a day to ask myself, *What am I feeling right now?* At first, my answers were vague and limited. Over time, they became more nuanced and specific.

I kept an emotion journal, connecting physical sensations with emotional states. The tightness in my chest wasn't just "stress"; it was anxiety about an upcoming presentation. The heaviness in my shoulders wasn't just "tiredness"; it was discouragement about a project delay. The clenched jaw wasn't just "tension"; it was resentment about being interrupted in meetings.

My therapist provided lists of emotional vocabulary that expanded my options beyond my usual three or four go-to terms. I learned to distinguish between similar but distinct feelings—between disappointment and defeat, between anxiety and anticipation, and between irritation and anger.

This process resembled learning any new skill: It felt awkward and forced at first. I consciously had to work at what seemed to come naturally to others. But with practice, greater fluency developed. What started as deliberate exercise gradually became more automatic.

Perhaps the most challenging aspect of taking off the mask was finding the courage to seek help—not just from a therapist, but from friends, family, and colleagues. This step challenged the deeply ingrained belief that independence equals strength and dependency indicates weakness—a false dichotomy that prevents many men from accessing needed support.

What ultimately helped me overcome this barrier was reframing help-seeking not as weakness, but as strategic resource utilization. Throughout my academic and management career, I tackled countless complex problems. I never hesitated to consult legal experts for regulatory issues or seek advice from IT professionals when facing a tech challenge. Why, then, should mental health be treated any differently?

During my MBA, I took leadership courses that focused heavily on understanding and motivating employees—how to recognize their mental states and cultivate a positive, productive work environment. But not once in all my schooling was there a meaningful emphasis on my own psychological well-being. We were trained to care for others' performance, yet rarely taught how to care for the mind that leads them. The human brain—its thoughts, emotions, and behaviors—is arguably the most complex system we have. Despite the advances of modern medicine, it remains one of the least understood organs. And yet, society expects us to cope with its dysfunction in silence.

What shifted things for me was recognizing that it's perfectly normal to start from ignorance. That's how we approach any new subject—we start with incompetence, then slowly build competence until mastery. I reminded myself of how I'd troubleshoot my phone when it malfunctioned: I'd look up expert videos, read articles, and, if needed, take it to a technician. And yet here I was, holding myself to the impossible standard of fixing my own brain, an organ far more complex than any phone, especially given the fact that the brain invented the phone in the first place.

So, why was I blaming myself for struggling? Why was I ashamed of not knowing what to do? What was truly stopping me from studying, understanding, and even mastering the fundamentals of my own mind?

The answers became clear: I should not blame myself, and I had no reason to feel ashamed. The only thing I "should" do was the best I could to understand what was happening. Because once you start to understand, even a little, it becomes easier to accept. That might sound simple, but in reality, it was anything but. It was a grueling, uphill battle. And while I can't claim I've fully completed that journey, I learned something just as important: You don't need to finish the process to feel its impact.

Just "being in" the process—acknowledging the issue, exploring it, and seeking understanding—was immensely helpful. I no longer woke up consumed by frustration and confusion, drifting without direction. I had a plan. It wasn't perfect, and it didn't guarantee instant relief—but it gave me structure, intention, and hope. And for the first time in a long while, that was enough to help me take the next step.

I wish I could say I talked to my friends and family, that they understood, and that everything turned out perfectly. But it didn't. How could I talk comfortably about something I barely understood myself?

Think about it: When you're going out to meet people, you shower, brush your teeth, get dressed, and maybe take a final look in the mirror to make sure you're presentable. You prepare your outer self to be seen. But when my mental health struggles began showing, when they started spilling out beyond my control, it felt like I had a new face entirely. A different version of me was stepping out into the world. And I didn't know if that version would be accepted. Hell, I didn't even know if I accepted it.

It was nerve-wracking. What would people think? Would they see me as unstable? Unreliable? Unrecognizable? I began to fear the loss of connection, the slow withdrawal of people who once enjoyed being around me. And I wondered, *If showing my true self meant someone didn't want to be around me anymore, what did that say about the relationship? Maybe that person wasn't really a friend to me, just to the mask I had worn. And how is that any different from someone who only likes you for your money, status, or usefulness at work?*

The truth is, the "new me" didn't lose everything. Yes, I lost some relationships, but I also gained others. People I barely knew, or who had only been acquaintances, showed up with a kind of compassion and honesty I hadn't expected. The experience opened new doors and reminded me that evolving is a natural part of life. And as we evolve, our relationships shift, too. That's why most people aren't still friends with their kindergarten classmates. Change is part of being human. And growth, especially the kind born from pain, reveals who truly sees you.

The noise in your head gets much quieter when you no longer have to pretend to be someone you're not.

BUILDING EMOTIONAL RESILIENCE: THE FOUNDATION OF LASTING STRENGTH

Six months after my breakdown, I stood in my therapist's office for what would be our last regular session. I wasn't "cured"—depression doesn't work that way—but I had the tools I needed to continue my journey.

"What's the most important thing you've learned here?" she asked.

I thought about all we'd discussed—the grief work, the cognitive techniques, and the mindfulness practices. But one insight stood above the rest.

Experiences open new doors and remind you that evolving is a natural part of life. And as we grow, our relationships shift, too

"I've learned that being strong doesn't mean never falling," I said finally. "It means knowing how to get back up and that sometimes, the getting-up part requires reaching for someone's hand."

She smiled. "That's resilience. And it will serve you better than any armor ever could."

When I walked out of her office that day, I wasn't the same man who had stumbled in six months earlier, unable to speak through my tears. I wasn't magically free of challenges or negative emotions. But I had something more valuable: the ability to face those challenges without being destroyed by them.

This wasn't the brittle strength I'd spent decades cultivating, the kind that looked impressive until it shattered completely. This was something flexible, adaptable, and renewable. Something that bent without breaking.

Emotional resilience, the capacity to adapt to stress and adversity while maintaining psychological well-being, is perhaps the most critical resource for men recovering from depression and fighting life's inevitable challenges. It's the difference between being knocked down by life's storms and being able to weather them—perhaps not without damage, but without being completely uprooted.

Let's be real: Most of us grew up thinking being tough meant hiding our feelings. But actual resilience isn't about bottling everything up; it's about facing your problems head-on while staying flexible enough to deal with them effectively, not just reacting on impulse.

And here's the thing: Resilience isn't some magical trait people are born with. It's more like a muscle you can build over time. For guys, especially, who've been told all their lives that controlling emotions equals strength, developing real resilience means two things: ditching the unhealthy coping mechanisms we've relied on, and learning better ways to handle life's challenges.

My own rebuilding process started with the simplest but most challenging practice: basic mindfulness. My therapist taught me to sit quietly for just five minutes each morning, noticing my breath and observing thoughts and feelings without immediately trying to fix or change them.

At first, I was terrible at it. My mind raced with to-do lists, work worries, and self-criticism. But, gradually, I developed the ability to notice my emotional weather patterns without immediately being swept away by them. I learned to say, "I'm experiencing anxiety right now," rather than "I am anxious," a subtle but powerful distinction that created space between me and my emotions.

This growing awareness laid the foundation for another crucial skill: cognitive restructuring. I realized how my thinking patterns contributed to my overthinking trap. Catastrophic thinking ("I'll never find another good job"), all-or-nothing perspectives ("I'm a complete failure"), and mind-reading ("Everyone thinks I'm incompetent") dominated my internal dialogue.

Learning to recognize and challenge these patterns didn't happen overnight. It involved catching myself in these thought spirals and asking questions like, "Is this actually true? What evidence supports or contradicts this thought? What would I tell a friend who was thinking this way?"

Gradually, I developed the ability to consider alternative perspectives. Not blind optimism—that would have felt false and unsustainable—but more balanced and realistic assessments of situations. This cognitive flexibility reduced the mental noise that had been consuming so much of my energy.

Perhaps most empowering was connecting daily actions to larger values—what some might call meaning-making. Depression had stripped life of its meaning, leaving me going through motions without purpose. Rediscovering what mattered to me, being present for my son, contributing something worthwhile through my work, and creating space for genuine connection gave me reasons to keep moving forward, even on difficult days.

I started asking myself each morning, *What small thing can I do today that aligns with what matters most?* Some days it was as simple as really listening to my son's stories about school instead of just nodding absently. Other days, it meant taking a small risk at work by sharing an idea I believed in. These weren't grand gestures, but they reconnected me to a sense of purpose that depression had stolen.

The final crucial element was the one I'd resisted most: intentionally building supportive relationships. The old version of me had prided himself on rarely needing others. The resilient version understood that human connection isn't a weakness but a biological necessity, as essential to psychological health as food and water are to physical survival.

I started small, reaching out to one trusted friend for coffee. Then I joined a men's support group where, for the first time, I heard other men speak honestly about struggles similar to mine. Eventually, I even organized a monthly dinner with colleagues where conversations gradually deepened beyond work topics.

These practices—mindfulness, cognitive flexibility, purpose-driven action, and social connection—worked together synergistically. They increased both my emotional awareness (the ability to recognize what I was feeling) and emotional regulation (the ability to experience feelings without being controlled by them).

What amazed me was how these practices, with regular repetition, eventually became more automatic. Just as physical training develops muscle memory, emotional resilience training builds neural pathways that make healthier responses more accessible. What had initially required conscious effort gradually became my new default.

Of course, I encountered plenty of barriers along the way. Perfectionism was a major obstacle. I expected immediate mastery of these skills and interpreted setbacks as failures. Learning to view resilience as a practice rather than a destination was itself a challenge. My difficulty distinguishing between what I could and couldn't control led to wasted energy on unwinnable battles while neglecting areas where I could make a difference.

Perhaps the most persistent barrier was my ingrained resistance to reaching out during difficult times. I'd been conditioned to see independence as a virtue and asking for help as a weakness. Recognizing how this traditional masculine socialization created vulnerability rather than strength was a painful but necessary insight. Men who won't ask for directions usually won't ask for help with their feelings, either.

Building emotional resilience didn't make me immune to life's challenges. I still have difficult days. I still experience anxiety, sadness, and frustration. But now, these emotions pass through me rather than define me. The overthinking that once trapped me in endless spirals has been replaced by a more compassionate and balanced internal voice.

When I look back at the man I was before—rigidly armored yet internally fragile—I feel compassion rather than judgment. He was doing the best he could with the tools he had. But I wouldn't trade the resilience I've developed for that brittle strength, not for anything.

True strength isn't about never falling or never feeling pain. It's about developing the capacity to face life's inevitable storms without being destroyed by them. It's about having the flexibility to bend without breaking. It's about knowing how to find your way back to solid ground when the winds have passed.

And sometimes—often, actually—it's about reaching for someone's hand as you get back up.

True strength isn't about never falling or never feeling pain. It's about developing the capacity to face life's inevitable storms without being destroyed by them.

CHAPTER 3:
THE BODY'S WISDOM— HOW PHYSICAL WELL-BEING NURTURES MENTAL HEALTH

Take care of your body.
It's the only place you have to live.

–JIM ROHN

The morning I first noticed the noise in my head had quieted, I was swimming.

Not competitively or even particularly well—just moving through water, back and forth across the pool. I hadn't planned this as therapy. In fact, I'd only started swimming because my therapist had gently but persistently suggested that adding some physical activity to my routine "might help."

I was skeptical. How could something as simple as exercise make any difference to the complex tangle of grief, depression, and anxiety that had overtaken my life? The overthinking that plagued me seemed too powerful, too entrenched in my mind to be affected by something as basic as moving my body.

Yet there I was, on my eighth lap, when I suddenly realized the constant chatter in my brain—the endless loop of worries, regrets, and fears—had temporarily stopped. My mind wasn't empty; it was simply... quiet. Present. Focused only on the rhythm of my breathing, the pull of my arms through water, and the gentle resistance against my skin.

The relief was so deep that I stopped midlap, my feet finding the bottom of the pool as I stood there, dripping and breathless, struck by this unexpected moment of mental peace.

It lasted perhaps three minutes before my thoughts began their familiar spiral again. But those three minutes of quiet showed me something crucial: My mind and body weren't separate systems operating independently. They were deeply, fundamentally connected.

THE MIND-BODY CONNECTION: YOUR BODY AS AN ALLY IN HEALING

For most of my life, I thought of my body and mind as separate systems—like neighboring countries that occasionally traded goods but largely operated independently. My mind was where the "real me" lived, while my body was just the vehicle that carried my brain from meeting to meeting.

This artificial division became most obvious during my deepest depression. While I recognized my mental suffering, I completely missed how my physical state was both reflecting and reinforcing my psychological distress. The chronic headaches, constant fatigue, digestive issues, and insomnia seemed like unrelated problems, annoying physical distractions from my "real" mental health issues.

My first hint that this division was an illusion came during that morning swim. The temporary mental quiet I experienced wasn't magic or a coincidence; it was biology at work. My body wasn't just responding to my mind; it was actively shaping it.

The connection between physical and mental wellness goes far deeper than we typically recognize. It's not just that exercise makes you feel good or that junk food can make you sluggish. What's happening involves complex relationships working through multiple biological systems in your body—your immune system, hormones, gut health, and neural pathways are all constantly influencing your mental state.

THE BODY: MOVEMENT

Let's start with movement. When I first started swimming regularly, I wasn't doing it to fix my brain chemistry; I was just following my therapist's suggestion to "get moving somehow." But with each lap, remarkable things were happening inside my body. My muscles were releasing proteins that traveled to my brain, promoting growth and repair of neural tissue. My heart was pumping more blood to my brain, delivering more oxygen and nutrients. My body was triggering the release of natural mood-elevating compounds that work very similarly to antidepressant medications.

One of the most important of these compounds has a complicated name—"brain-derived neurotrophic factor" (BDNF)—but its function is straightforward: It helps your brain grow and adapt. Think of it as fertilizer for your brain cells. During depression, BDNF levels typically drop, making it harder for your brain to maintain healthy neural connections. Regular physical activity boosts BDNF levels, giving your brain the resources it needs to heal and adapt.

This isn't just theory. Studies have found that consistent moderate exercise can be as effective as antidepressant medication for many people with mild to moderate depression (Noetel et al., 2024). Some research even shows that people who include regular exercise in their recovery have lower relapse rates compared with those using medication alone (Al-Qahtani et al., 2018).

For me, as for many men, physical activity provided a comfortable starting point for broader wellness practices. When I couldn't yet face talking about my feelings, I could face a swim workout. Moving my body felt productive and in keeping with masculine norms in a way that other aspects of mental health care didn't initially. It became my gateway to healing.

THE BODY: NUTRITION

The food we eat plays an equally crucial role in mental health, something I discovered when my therapist suggested meeting with a nutritionist as part of my recovery plan. I was skeptical (again), but I agreed to try.

What I learned surprised me. The standard American diet I'd been eating for years—loaded with processed foods, sugar, and inflammatory oils— wasn't just affecting my waistline; it was potentially fueling my depression. These foods increase inflammation throughout the body, including the brain, and inflammation has strong links to depression and anxiety (Kim et al., 2022).

By contrast, diets rich in whole foods, healthy fats (especially omega-3s found in fish), and plenty of plants are associated with lower depression rates (Grosso et al., 2014). When I gradually shifted toward this eating pattern—not perfectly, but consistently—I noticed improvements in both my energy levels and mood stability.

The nutritionist explained that these effects work partly through what scientists call the gut-brain axis, a two-way communication system between your digestive tract and your central nervous system. Your gut bacteria actually produce about 95% of your body's serotonin, a neurotransmitter crucial for mood regulation (Appleton, 2018). This means your digestive health directly impacts your mental wellness.

THE BODY: SLEEP

Sleep quality showed the most immediate connection to my daily mental state. During my worst depression, I either couldn't sleep at all or would sleep for ten hours and still wake up exhausted. This wasn't just an annoyance; it was actively making my depression worse.

Sleep disruption alters emotional regulation, cognitive function, and stress-response systems. Without adequate quality sleep, your brain becomes more vulnerable to negative thought patterns and less capable of the cognitive flexibility needed to break out of overthinking cycles. For men specifically, sleep disorders frequently accompany depression, each making the other worse in a challenging cycle.

When I finally addressed my sleep issues through consistent bedtime routines, creating a proper sleep environment (cool, dark, and quiet), reducing evening screen time, and practicing relaxation techniques before bed, I gained more stable ground for all my other recovery efforts.

What makes the mind-body connection so powerful is its bidirectional nature. Just as mental states like depression or anxiety can trigger physical symptoms, improving physical wellness creates positive ripples in your mental health. This creates the possibility of positive cycles replacing negative ones.

I experienced this firsthand. Better sleep gave me more energy for exercise. Regular exercise improved my sleep quality. Both made healthier eating easier to maintain. Better nutrition supported more stable energy and mood. These mutually reinforcing benefits created momentum that made recovery feel increasingly possible rather than overwhelming.

UNDERSTANDING THE WEIGHT WE CARRY: STRESS AND BURNOUT IN MEN'S LIVES

The night before my breakdown in the telemarketing cubicle, I sat in my car in the empty parking lot, unable to start the engine and drive home. It was nearly midnight. I'd stayed late again, making call after call, chasing numbers that never seemed good enough, trying to prove my worth in a job I secretly hated.

My phone buzzed with a text from my wife:

Everything okay?

I typed back:

Fine. Just wrapping up. Home soon.

But I wasn't fine. My hands were shaking. My chest felt tight. The thought of returning the next morning filled me with a dread so intense it felt like physical pain. Still, I couldn't name what was happening. In my mind, this was just normal work stress—something to power through, to overcome through sheer force of will, like I always had.

I didn't recognize these as warning signs. I didn't see the flames before the fire.

Looking back now, I can identify that moment as the final stage of burnout, the culmination of years carrying a weight that had grown so gradually I hardly noticed how it was crushing me. If I had understood then what I know now about stress, burnout, and their effects on the mind and body, perhaps I could have prevented what came next.

The truth is that most men today carry a weight of stress that our bodies and minds were never designed to bear. The professional demands of modern work create a state of chronic stress unlike anything our ancestors experienced. Technology has eliminated the natural boundaries between work and personal life. Emails, texts, and calls follow us everywhere. The "workday" never truly ends.

During my banking career, I was expected to be available around the clock. The BlackBerry (yes, I'm dating myself here) sat on my nightstand, and I'd reflexively check it if I awoke during the night. Vacations were punctuated by "just checking in" calls. Weekends were for "catching up" on work. There was always more to do, always someone working harder, always the fear of falling behind.

For men whose identity remains heavily tied to professional achievement—and despite cultural shifts, this describes most of us—these pressures carry particular psychological weight. Our sense of worth becomes entangled with our performance, our status, and our ability to provide and succeed. This creates a dangerous situation where stress isn't just uncomfortable—it becomes threatening to our very sense of self.

The competitive environments many men work in further compound this stress. We constantly compare ourselves to colleagues, worry about status, and fear replacement or obsolescence. During my banking years, each quarterly performance review generated weeks of anxiety beforehand and either temporary relief or deepened insecurity afterward. The next review was always looming, creating a cycle of pressure that never fully subsided.

Without adequate recovery periods, this chronic activation of our stress-response systems depletes physical and psychological resources. It's like running a car engine at high RPMs without ever allowing it to cool down. Eventually, something is going to break. That breaking point is burnout, a state of chronic stress characterized by emotional exhaustion, cynicism, and reduced professional efficacy.

By the time I found myself sitting in that parking lot, unable to move, I had hit all three markers: I felt emotionally hollow, deeply cynical about my work and its meaning, and convinced of my incompetence despite objective evidence to the contrary. But I still didn't recognize it as burn-out. In my mind, burnout was for people who couldn't handle pressure, and I prided myself on being someone who could handle anything.

This denial was fueled by societal expectations that create additional pres-sure through mixed messages about male roles and identity. As men today, we're expected to embody contradictory qualities—to be ambitious career builders and present, engaged fathers; competitive in the workplace but col-laborative team players; and traditionally masculine but emotionally evolved.

These impossible standards create what psychologists call "role strain," persistent stress from attempting to fulfill incompatible expectations (Nickerson, 2023). I felt this acutely after my first son was born, torn between my identity as an ambitious professional and my desire to be a more present father than mine had been. Whatever choice I made in any given moment, I felt I was failing at something important.

Adding to this burden, many of us feel pressure to conceal our stress symptoms, viewing stress admission as weakness rather than as appro-priate recognition of human limitations. I became masterful at projecting calm competence while inwardly crumbling. This concealment prevented early intervention that might have helped me recognize and address my deteriorating condition before it culminated in a complete breakdown.

What I didn't understand then was how deeply chronic stress was affect-ing me physically. The constant elevation of stress hormones, such as cortisol, was disrupting my sleep, impairing my cognitive function, sup-pressing my immune system, and contributing to headaches and chest pain I attributed to "just getting older." These physical effects created a physiological environment highly conducive to depression development, helping explain my rapid progression from burnout to clinical depression.

The psychological effects were equally devastating. I experienced what experts call "cognitive narrowing," a decreased ability to see options or possibilities (David, 2023). Problems that once would have sparked creative solutions now seemed insurmountable. My emotional resources were depleted to the point where even small difficulties felt overwhelming. I began emotionally detaching from work and relationships, going through motions without genuine engagement. Perhaps most painfully, I lost any sense of accomplishment or effectiveness. No achievement, however significant, could penetrate the conviction that I was fundamentally failing.

These effects further diminished my resilience, creating vulnerability to deepening psychological distress. The overthinking that had always been part of my personality morphed into something darker and more paralyzing—endless rumination without resolution, worry without relief.

Had someone told me a year earlier that I was heading for this cliff edge, I wouldn't have believed them. I was just doing what men are supposed to do—working hard, providing for my family, and handling things without complaint. I didn't see how unsustainable my pace had become. I didn't recognize how the weight I carried was reshaping not just my mind but my brain and body.

MOVEMENT AS MEDICINE: FINDING YOUR PATH TO PHYSICAL WELLNESS

When my therapist first suggested I start exercising to help with my depression, I nearly laughed out loud. My mind was broken—how could sweating fix that? Besides, I had memories of high school gym class and military-style boot camps that made "exercise" seem about as appealing as a root canal.

"I'm not asking you to become a bodybuilder," she said, noticing my reluctance. "Just find some way to move your body that doesn't make you miserable. Do it consistently. See what happens."

Her modest proposal felt doable, so I tried swimming—partly because it seemed gentler than running and partly because I could be alone with no one watching me gasp for breath. The first few sessions were uncomfortable. My lungs burned. My arms felt like wet noodles afterward. But something kept me coming back.

Three weeks in, during that aforementioned ordinary Tuesday morning swim, the constant noise in my head—the overthinking that had been my constant companion—temporarily quieted. For just a few precious minutes, my mind was as clear as the water around me. That moment of peace was worth more than any muscle I might build or pound I might lose.

I tell this story not to promote swimming specifically, but to illustrate a broader truth: Movement isn't just medicine for your body; it's medicine for your mind. And finding the right movement for you might be one of the most important steps in your journey out of depression and overthinking.

Creating a sustainable fitness routine isn't about forcing yourself into some idealized regimen you saw in a magazine or punishing your body to compensate for perceived failings. You're looking for alignment with your individual preferences, capacities, and goals. For men recovering from depression, the psychological benefits often exceed the physical benefits, making consistency far more important than intensity.

The keyword here is *consistent*. A single intense workout won't fix depression, just like a single therapy session won't resolve complex emotional issues. It's the regular practice that rewires your brain over time, gradually shifting your neurochemistry and thought patterns.

Finding activities that generate either enjoyment or a sense of accomplishment will increase your chances of sticking with them long-term. Some men prefer the meditative aspects of solo activities like running, cycling, or swimming—opportunities to be alone with their thoughts in a structured way that prevents rumination. Others benefit more from the social connection and accountability of team sports or group fitness classes, where the camaraderie provides additional mental health benefits.

Movement isn't just medicine for your body; it's medicine for your mind.

Start with modest, achievable goals and gradually increase duration or intensity as your capacity grows. I began with just 15 minutes of swimming, 3 times a week. It wasn't impressive, but it was doable, and that made all the difference. Starting too ambitiously often leads to discouragement that derails fitness attempts before the benefits can take hold.

Alongside movement, nutrition plays a crucial role in mental health, something I discovered largely through trial and error after my initial breakthrough with exercise. The food you eat isn't just fuel for your muscles; it provides the raw materials your brain needs to function optimally and regulate your mood.

Effective nutrition strategies for improving mental health focus on three key areas: reducing inflammation (which is linked to depression), supporting neurotransmitter production, and stabilizing blood sugar to prevent the mood swings that come with glucose fluctuations.

In practical terms, this means

- Emphasizing omega-3-rich foods like fatty fish, walnuts, and flaxseeds that reduce inflammation and support brain cell function
- Including fermented foods like yogurt, kimchi, or sauerkraut that support gut health and the microbiome diversity linked to serotonin production
- Ensuring adequate protein intake, which provides the building blocks for neurotransmitters
- Consuming complex carbohydrates (like those in oats, sweet potatoes, and legumes) that stabilize blood sugar
- Minimizing processed foods, especially those containing industrial seed oils and refined sugars that promote inflammation

I found that rather than pursuing perfect adherence to some restrictive diet plan, sustainable improvement came through gradually increasing the nutritious foods while reducing the inflammatory ones. Small, consistent changes were far more effective than dramatic overhauls I couldn't maintain.

For many men, myself included, framing nutrition in terms of performance optimization rather than restriction increases motivation. I wasn't giving up certain foods because they were "bad"; I was giving them up because they were interfering with how well my brain and body functioned. This subtle shift made healthier choices feel empowering rather than depriving.

The final piece of the physical wellness puzzle—and perhaps the most immediately impactful—is sleep. During my worst depression, sleep was either elusive or excessive but never restorative. Addressing this single factor made everything else in my recovery more manageable.

Sleep-quality improvement begins with consistency, maintaining regular sleep and wake-up times that allow sufficient duration (typically 7–9 hours for adults). Our bodies thrive on rhythms and patterns. Going to bed and waking up at roughly the same times each day, even on weekends, helps regulate your internal clock.

Environmental optimization matters, too. Keep your bedroom dark, quiet, and cool. Remove electronic devices that emit sleep-disrupting blue light or, at minimum, use night mode settings. Create pre-sleep routines that signal to your body the transition from wakefulness to sleep—perhaps reading, gentle stretching, or a warm shower.

Practical habits that support better sleep include limiting caffeine after midday, restricting substances (which might help you fall asleep but disrupt the deep, restorative stages), and avoiding late meals that can cause discomfort or energy surges when you're trying to wind down.

For the many men who struggle with persistent sleep difficulties, approaches like cognitive behavioral therapy for insomnia (CBT-I) show better long-term results than sleep medications. These techniques address the thought patterns and behaviors that perpetuate sleep problems rather than temporarily forcing sleep through chemical means.

I also discovered the value of intentional rest periods throughout the day, even brief 5–10 minute breaks from focused attention. These micro-recoveries help regulate stress hormones and prevent the hyperarousal that often disrupts sleep later. A short walk around the block, a few minutes of deep breathing, or even just gazing out the window can provide these beneficial pauses.

Movement, nutrition, and sleep form a three-legged stool that supports mental wellness. Each enhances the other in a virtuous cycle. Better sleep gives you energy for movement, and regular movement improves sleep quality. Both make healthier eating choices easier. Nutritious eating supports energy for movement and biochemistry for good sleep.

You don't need to perfect all three simultaneously. Start where you feel most drawn or where you suspect you'll see the quickest benefits. For me, movement opened the door, with sleep and nutrition improvements following naturally as I began feeling the positive effects of regular activity.

The body has wisdom that the overthinking mind often lacks. Learning to listen to and care for your physical self isn't separate from mental health recovery. It's an essential foundation that makes all other healing possible.

DAILY PRACTICES FOR CALM AND BALANCE: TAMING THE STRESS RESPONSE

The first time I recognized what was happening in my mind, I had just finished studying for the day for my CPA exam and lay down in bed. I started thinking about what portion I'd tackle the next day. Then I calculated, based on my pace, when I might finish the entire review. So, I tried to reflect on how much I'd studied that day and what I'd actually comprehended. My mind went blank. I could not remember a single thing I'd studied just hours earlier.

My heart started racing. If I couldn't recall material from the same day, how would I possibly remember it months from now on test day? My jaw clenched so tight it hurt. Inside my head, a familiar voice was working overtime:

You're retaining nothing. All these hours hunched over books, and for what? You'll never be ready in time. Everyone else is probably flying through this material. You're going to fail the exam, waste all this money, and have to explain to everyone why you couldn't cut it. Your whole career plan will collapse...

I was just spitting out one negative thought after another, and it was like a whole movie played in my head in mere seconds.

Suddenly, I started realizing what was happening; it felt so familiar. But this time was different; usually, I was just a passenger on a train headed off a cliff. And the only thing I could do was ride through the motion and follow it to the bottom of the valley until I went through the process of waking up after the crash. And start the recovery process by climbing out of the wreckage, dragging myself all the way out of the valley to the road.

It was like I could see a gauge, like a speedometer, measuring my state of mind rapidly approaching the red zone, and I was just waiting for the cycle to complete itself. I was but a second away from an anxiety attack.

In the middle of the chaos, I heard another voice. It was like hearing myself hushing my son when he was crying excessively. *Hush, not another thought. Just get out of bed and wash your face. You can always get back to your thought process if you want, but stop for a second and wash your face.* So, I got up and washed my face, and then I thought, *I'm not in a rush to continue this spiral, so let me go to the kitchen and get a cup of milk.* I walked around the house sipping from the cup while my thinking started: *keep stalling as much as you want, but eventually, you must go back to bed and be alone with your thoughts.*

I took a deep breath and, for the first time, questioned these thoughts instead of accepting them as reality. Was it true that I had "completely bombed" that day? Well, I'd studied for at least 10 hours. My comprehension might not have been great, and at that moment, I couldn't recall what I'd studied, but that wasn't the end of the world. I would review the material multiple times anyway. And it was late; the following morning might be a better time to review the plan and timeline, whereas now it was time to get some rest because it was really the only thing I could do

As I challenged each thought with actual evidence, the physical symptoms—the racing heart, the tight jaw—gradually subsided. The thoughts didn't disappear completely, but they lost their iron grip on my body and emotions. A small space opened up between stimulus and response, between thought and reaction. In that space, I found the first hint of freedom from the overthinking trap.

This approach, systematically identifying and challenging stress-promoting thought patterns, is at the heart of cognitive behavioral techniques that have helped millions break free from anxiety, depression, and chronic stress. These practical tools don't require special equipment or hours of daily practice, just a willingness to turn toward your thoughts with curiosity rather than accepting them as unchangeable truth.

The process begins with recognizing the automatic thoughts that amplify your stress response. These often follow predictable patterns:

- **Catastrophizing:** *This presentation will be a complete disaster.*

- **Overgeneralizing:** *I always freeze up when the pressure's on.*

- **Mind-reading:** *My boss thinks I'm not cut out for this promotion.*

- **Black-and-white thinking:** *Either I nail this perfectly, or I'm a failure.*

Once you identify these patterns, the practice involves examining evidence for and against these thoughts, generating alternative interpretations, and developing more balanced perspectives.

For me, this meant keeping a small notebook where I wrote down particularly stressful thoughts as they occurred. At the end of each day, I'd pick one or two to examine more closely. What evidence supported this thought? What evidence contradicted it? What would I tell a friend who expressed this same thought about himself? Gradually, I developed the habit of questioning my thoughts rather than immediately believing them.

This cognitive restructuring reduces emotional reactivity and creates psychological space for more effective problem-solving. It doesn't eliminate stress entirely—nor should it, since stress has valuable functions—but it prevents stress from spiraling into overthinking and paralysis.

For many men, myself included, the logical, evidence-based nature of cognitive behavioral approaches feels accessible and practical compared to more open-ended therapeutic approaches. It appeals to our problem-solving orientation and gives us concrete tools we can apply immediately.

Alongside these cognitive techniques, I discovered the power of mindfulness practices, though not without initial resistance. When my therapist first suggested mindfulness, I pictured incense-burning meditation sessions and immediately balked. "I'm not really into that spiritual stuff," I told her.

"Forget the images you have of meditation," she replied. "Think of it as attention training—like going to the gym, but for your focus muscles."

That reframing made all the difference. I started with simple practices: five minutes each morning focusing on my breath, noticing when my mind wandered (which it did constantly at first), and gently bringing attention back without self-criticism. Later, I added mindful walking during lunch breaks, paying attention to the physical sensations of each step rather than ruminating on work problems.

These practices develop the capacity to notice thoughts and feelings without immediate reactivity, a crucial skill for breaking automatic stress patterns and creating space for intentional responses.

For men accustomed to an external focus, mindfulness practices initially require significant effort but yield increasing returns as capacity develops. The key is consistency rather than duration—five minutes daily builds more capacity than an hour once a week.

The final piece that helped me tame my overactive stress response was creating structured daily routines. When depression disrupted my normal functioning, having clear routines provided psychological scaffolding that supported recovery. These routines balanced productivity, connection, physical activity, and restoration in rhythms that honored both my energy cycles and obligations.

My morning routine proved particularly powerful for setting psychological patterns for the day. Before touching my phone or checking email, I would:

- Drink a full glass of water.
- Stretch or do a brief workout.
- Eat something with protein.
- Spend five minutes writing down my main priorities and connecting them to my values.

This simple sequence, which took less than 30 minutes total, created a buffer between sleep and the day's demands, allowing me to enter my workday from a centered place rather than immediately reacting to others' needs and emergencies.

Evening routines supported sleep quality through gradual disengagement from stimulating activities. I established a technology cut-off time (initially 9 p.m., later pushed back to 8 p.m.), after which I would avoid screens and transition toward more calming activities—reading, light stretching, or conversation with my wife. This created a gentle slope toward sleep rather than the cliff-edge I'd previously experienced, lying in bed wide awake with an activated mind unable to downshift.

These practices—cognitive restructuring, mindfulness, and structured routines—work together synergistically to tame the stress response that fuels overthinking. The cognitive work addresses the content of thoughts, mindfulness builds the capacity to relate differently to thoughts regardless of content, and routines create the environmental conditions that support both practices.

None of these approaches eliminated stress from my life entirely, nor would I want that. Stress itself isn't the enemy; it's a natural, sometimes helpful, response to life's challenges. What these practices did was change my relationship with stress from being controlled by it to working with it. They created space between stimulus and response, between pressure and reaction, and between stress and suffering.

In that space—small at first, but growing with practice—I found the beginning of freedom from the overthinking trap. The noise didn't disappear completely, but it no longer dominated my inner landscape. For the first time in years, I could hear something else beneath the anxious chatter: my voice, clearer and calmer than I remembered it being.

These practices require no special talent or background, just consistent attention and a willingness to try approaches that might initially feel unfamiliar. The returns they offer in mental quiet, emotional balance, and freedom from overthinking make them among the most valuable investments you can make in your well-being.

CHAPTER 4:
THE AWAKENING PATH— FINDING MEANING AFTER CRISIS

Amor fati – "Love your fate,"
which is in fact your life.
–FRIEDRICH NIETZSCHE

Six months after my breakdown, I sat alone on a park bench watching my son play. The worst of my depression had lifted. The constant noise in my head had quieted to a manageable hum. The physical symptoms that had plagued me—the headaches, the chest tightness, the insomnia—had largely subsided. By most measures, I was recovering.

Yet, something was still missing.

I had learned tools to manage my overthinking. I had rebuilt daily routines that supported my mental health. I had even begun to understand the roots of my depression in ways that made me feel less broken and more human. But a question kept surfacing: What now? What was I recovering from?

Without a clear answer, I felt like a car with a repaired engine but no destination: functional but purposeless. The overthinking that had once consumed me with worry now circled around this existential vacuum. What was the point of getting better if I was just returning to the same life that had led to my collapse?

That afternoon in the park, watching my son's uninhibited joy as he climbed and ran and imagined, a thought struck me with unexpected clarity: *Perhaps the breakdown wasn't just an ending but also a beginning.* Perhaps it had cleared away what wasn't working to make space for something new to emerge.

This realization marked the start of what I've come to call the awakening path—the journey from merely functioning again to finding genuine meaning and purpose in the aftermath of crisis. It's the difference between surviving and truly living, between existence and engagement, and between noise reduction and actual fulfillment.

THE SACRED JOURNEY THROUGH LOSS

The email confirmation from the university arrived on a Tuesday morning, exactly eight months after my sister's funeral and six months after my breakdown in the telemarketing cubicle. I'd been accepted into the Master's in Accounting program, a complete departure from my banking career and telemarketing detour.

I expected to feel excitement or at least relief. Instead, I felt a strange mixture of emptiness and apprehension. This should have been a moment of celebration, of forward momentum. Yet, as I stared at the acceptance letter on my screen, the question that had been haunting me for months resurfaced: "What's the point of any of this?"

The banking career I'd built my identity around was gone. My sister, whose fierce intelligence had always inspired me, was gone. The confident, ambitious person I'd thought myself to be had vanished somewhere

Perhaps the breakdown wasn't just an ending but also a beginning.

between grief and depression. Who was I now? What was I working toward? Why did anything matter?

These weren't just symptoms of depression lingering, though my therapist initially treated them that way. They were genuine philosophical questions bubbling up from a place deeper than mood, questions about meaning, purpose, and identity that demanded answers before I could truly move forward.

When traditional sources of meaning—career success, relationship roles, and physical capabilities, among others—are suddenly removed, we often experience what philosophers call an "existential vacuum," a deep emptiness and questioning of life's significance (Weininger, 2022). While painful, this crisis also creates an opportunity for examining previously unquestioned assumptions about what constitutes a meaningful life.

I had never questioned whether climbing the corporate ladder was meaningful. I had never examined whether my worth was truly connected to my job title or income. I had never considered whether the goals I was pursuing were actually mine or just expectations I'd absorbed from family and society. Loss stripped away these unexamined assumptions, forcing me to look at the scaffolding I'd built my life upon.

The psychiatrist Viktor Frankl, who survived Nazi concentration camps, observed something deep through his experiences: Those who maintained or discovered meaning amid extreme suffering demonstrated remarkably greater resilience than those who lost their sense of purpose, regardless of their physical conditions or resources (Frankl, 2018).

His insight resonated with my experience. When I was simply going through the motions of recovery—taking medication, attending therapy, and practicing the techniques—I made progress, but I still felt hollow. It was only when I began seriously wrestling with questions of meaning that something shifted inside me. The noise of overthinking began to organize itself around purpose rather than spinning in endless anxious circles.

The search for meaning provided a critical pathway out of depression's paralyzing hopelessness by reconnecting me with values and possibilities beyond my immediate suffering. This process involved both letting go of previous identity attachments and gradually discovering new sources of meaning that were less dependent on external validation or achievement metrics.

For me, this transition involved moving from meaning derived primarily through doing and achieving toward meaning discovered through being and connecting. I had always found purpose in accomplishment—closing deals, earning promotions, and achieving targets. Now, I was learning to find meaning in presence—being fully available in conversations with my kids, connecting authentically with my wife, and listening deeply to friends and classmates.

This shift didn't diminish my ambition or productivity but grounded it in deeper values beyond superficial success markers. My decision to pursue accounting came not from status considerations but from recognizing my genuine interest in creating order from numerical chaos and my desire for work that would provide stability for my family while respecting boundaries between work and home.

The search itself became therapeutic. As Nietzsche observed, "He who has a why to live can bear almost any how." Having meaningful goals made the difficult work of recovery feel worthwhile. The techniques for managing overthinking became not just survival tools but steps toward a life I actually wanted to live.

Perhaps most surprisingly, I found myself developing what researchers call "meaning-focused coping"—finding significance and purpose within suffering rather than despite it (Wang et al., 2019). My experiences with depression and grief, painful as they were, gave me insights and compassion I hadn't possessed before. I found myself able to connect with others in their struggles in ways my previously positive persona couldn't have managed.

This represents a crucial aspect of post-traumatic growth: the psychological development that can occur following a crisis or trauma. Rather than simply returning to my previous state, I was integrating my experiences into a new, more nuanced understanding of life and of myself.

For many men, discovering how their suffering enables them to help others facing similar challenges provides particularly powerful meaning. I found this to be true when I started occasionally sharing my experiences with fellow students who seemed to be struggling. These conversations—quiet, honest exchanges about difficulty and resilience—felt more meaningful than many of my previous "accomplishments."

EMBRACING SPIRITUALITY IN THE HEALING PROCESS

I grew up in a moderately religious household, the kind where we attended prayer once a week but rarely discussed faith during the week. By adulthood, I'd drifted away from organized religion, considering myself "spiritual but not religious" in that noncommittal way that requires little actual practice or commitment. My spirituality was like a neglected houseplant, technically alive but hardly thriving.

When depression hit, this vague spirituality offered little support. In the darkest moments, I had no spiritual vocabulary for my suffering, no practices to turn to, and no community to hold me. The overthinking that plagued me included existential questions I had no framework to address: Why was I suffering? What was the point of any of this? Was there any meaning to be found?

Three months into my recovery, I found myself sitting in a small room at a local meditation center. I wasn't there for spiritual reasons—my therapist had suggested meditation for stress management, and this Tuesday-night group was free. I arrived late, slipping into the back row, skeptical but desperate enough to try anything that might quiet my mind.

The teacher, a man about my age with kind eyes and no spiritual trappings beyond simple clothes, began with instructions so basic I couldn't mess them up: "Just notice your breath. When your mind wanders, gently bring it back. That's the whole practice."

For 20 minutes, I struggled to focus on my breath for even a few seconds before thoughts pulled me away. But in the brief moments when I managed to stay present, I experienced something remarkable: The constant noise in my head briefly ceased, replaced by a simple awareness of existing. Not thinking about existing, not worrying about existing, just... being.

That fleeting experience brought me back the following week. And the week after. Gradually, something shifted. The practice itself became a kind of spirituality—not through dogma or belief, but through direct experience of presence beyond my thinking mind.

This opened the door to a broader spiritual exploration that became central to my healing process. Spirituality—which I define simply as a connection to something larger than myself—provided resources for weathering depression and existential questioning that nothing else could match.

Research consistently shows correlations between spiritual practice and improved mental health outcomes, including lower depression rates, faster recovery, reduced suicide risk, and greater life satisfaction (Najafi et al., 2022). These benefits appear across diverse spiritual traditions, suggesting that the common elements of meaning-making, community connection, meditation or prayer, and ethical frameworks contribute more to mental health benefits than specific theological beliefs.

For men specifically, spiritual frameworks often provide permission to acknowledge vulnerability and suffering in contexts where such expression might otherwise feel unacceptable. In men's groups with spiritual foundations, I found myself able to speak about weakness, fear, and confusion in ways that would have felt impossible in purely secular male spaces.

Spirituality supported my mental health through a variety of psychological mechanisms. My growing spiritual practice provided a coherent meaning system that helped me interpret suffering not as random punishment but as part of human experience with potential for growth. It offered community support and belonging through the meditation group that eventually became important friends. The regular contemplative practice improved my emotional regulation, creating space between stimulus and response. And it provided ethical guidelines that helped me make decisions during periods when my internal compass felt broken.

The spiritual traditions I explored explicitly addressed suffering not as meaningless misery but as a potential catalyst for growth, wisdom, and compassion, a perspective that supported post-traumatic growth during my recovery. This reframing proved particularly valuable when finding meaning in suffering offered crucial momentum toward healing.

One concept that particularly resonated with me came from ancient Stoic philosophers and was later developed by Nietzsche: *amor fati*—learning to love one's fate. This doesn't suggest passive resignation to suffering but rather an active embrace of life exactly as it is, including its difficulties and disappointments.

When I first encountered this idea in a book someone from my meditation group recommended, it struck me as impossible, even offensive. Love my depression? Love my sister's death? Love losing my career? But as I sat with the concept, I began to understand its subtle wisdom.

Amor fati transformed the question from "Why did this happen to me?" to "How can I use this experience?" It didn't deny pain but integrated it into a larger narrative of personal development. It wasn't about pretending everything was fine but about accepting reality completely as the necessary starting point for any meaningful action.

This philosophical stance didn't immediately stop my overthinking, but it changed its quality. Instead of ruminating on how things should be different, I began contemplating how to work with things exactly as they were. The noise in my head became less frantic and more purposeful.

My spiritual journey wasn't about adopting specific religious beliefs. It was about developing practices that connected me to something beyond my individual struggles, whether I conceptualized that as God, the universe, human community, or simply a deeper dimension of experience. That connection provided perspective that made the overthinking mind seem less all-encompassing and its concerns less ultimate.

When I speak of embracing spirituality in the healing process, I'm not advocating for any particular tradition. I'm suggesting that finding some way to connect with what feels larger and more enduring than your immediate suffering can provide both comfort and orientation during the darkest times.

The specific form this takes matters less than the experience itself, of being part of something that transcends your individual pain while simultaneously honoring it as part of a meaningful human journey.

CREATING SMALL GOALS THAT BUILD MOMENTUM

The night before my first CPA exam, I sat at my kitchen table surrounded by study materials, gripped by a familiar panic. The overthinking had returned full force: *You're not ready. You'll fail. This whole accounting path is another mistake. Who are you kidding? You couldn't handle banking, and that was your specialty. How will you manage in a completely new field?*

The voices were so loud that I could barely focus on the practice problems in front of me. Then I noticed the wall calendar where I'd been tracking my study hours: four months of small, green checkmarks, each representing a two-hour study session completed. Three hundred and twenty hours of consistent effort, broken into manageable pieces, day after day after day.

I took a deep breath and felt something shift. The noise didn't disappear completely, but it faded enough for me to hear another voice: *You've prepared for this, step by step. You've done the work. Now, just take the next step.*

The next morning, I passed the first section of the CPA exam, not with a perfect score, but comfortably above the requirement. More importantly, I'd discovered something crucial about recovery: Structure and goals weren't just about achievement; they were lifelines pulling me forward when my own internal compass was still unreliable.

When I first entered the master's in accounting program, I was still struggling with depression's aftermath. My concentration came and went. My confidence had been shattered. My energy fluctuated wildly. What saved me wasn't inspiration or willpower—it was structure. The program provided external architecture that supported my functioning, even when internal resources faltered.

I learned to lean in to this structure by creating my own system of small, achievable goals that built momentum through consistent progress. Instead of focusing on the overwhelming endpoint (complete degree, pass all four CPA sections, secure position at accounting firm), I broke everything down into next actions that felt doable even on my worst days.

This structure operated through multiple mechanisms. It provided clear direction when my internal guidance felt absent. I didn't have to decide what mattered each day; I just had to follow the plan. It created accountability through external commitments: study groups, assignment deadlines, and exam dates. It broke overwhelming challenges into manageable steps: "read chapter 3" instead of "understand all of tax law." And it generated visible evidence of progress that counteracted depression's distorted perception that I was going nowhere.

For me, as for many men, structured goals offered comfortable familiarity with achievement-oriented approaches while simultaneously supporting recovery. Goal-setting was familiar territory; I'd always been good at pursuing targets in my professional life. Now, I was using that same skill for healing, creating new, smaller goals that would eventually lead me out of depression's depths.

What surprised me most were the psychological benefits beyond mere accomplishment. Each completed goal, however small, triggered satisfaction that temporarily elevated mood. Over time, these accumulated experiences rebuilt my belief in the connection between effort and reward, a connection that depression had severed. Where depression had convinced me that nothing I did mattered or made a difference, each checkmark on my calendar argued otherwise.

Documented progress challenged depression's lies about my capability and worth. When the voice in my head said, *You're a failure*, my completed assignments said otherwise. When it whispered, *You'll never manage this*, my past exams contradicted it with evidence. This evidence-based approach to challenging negative thoughts resonated with my analytical mind in ways that pure positive thinking never could.

Professional development provided me with a particularly effective recovery structure. While focusing exclusively on work can become unhealthy avoidance, thoughtfully integrated professional goals gave me a valuable framework. My accounting studies combined meaningful challenge with cultural acceptability. No one questioned my dedication to a degree program, making it socially safer than some other recovery activities.

I learned to create effective professional goals with specific character-istics. They were consistent with my genuine values (financial stability, intellectual challenge, clear boundaries between work and home) rather than external expectations (status, wealth, power). They included pro-cess metrics I could control ("study two hours daily") rather than solely outcome metrics ("get an A"). They incorporated regular feedback through quizzes and assignments that allowed adjustment before major exams. And they balanced challenge with achievability, stretching me without overwhelming me.

This balance transformed professional development from a potential stressor to a recovery asset. The new goals provided external structure while my internal systems healed. The overthinking that had once spi-raled endlessly now had channels to flow through: productive problems to solve, concrete challenges to address, and clear actions to take.

The smaller-goal approach extended beyond academics and career. I applied the same principle to rebuilding relationships, physical fitness, and spiritual practices. In each area, I identified the smallest meaningful action I could take consistently, then built on that foundation one step at a time.

The momentum created by this approach became self-reinforcing. Each completed step increased my capacity for the next one. The evidence of progress bolstered my belief that further progress was possible. The noise of overthinking gradually subsided as my mind engaged with defined, meaningful challenges rather than spinning in anxious circles.

Four years after beginning this journey, I stood at my CPA certification ceremony, all four exam sections passed, with a position at a midsized accounting firm secured. But the real achievement wasn't the professional credential; it was the path of goals I'd created and followed, one small goal at a time, that led from depression's darkness into a life worth living.

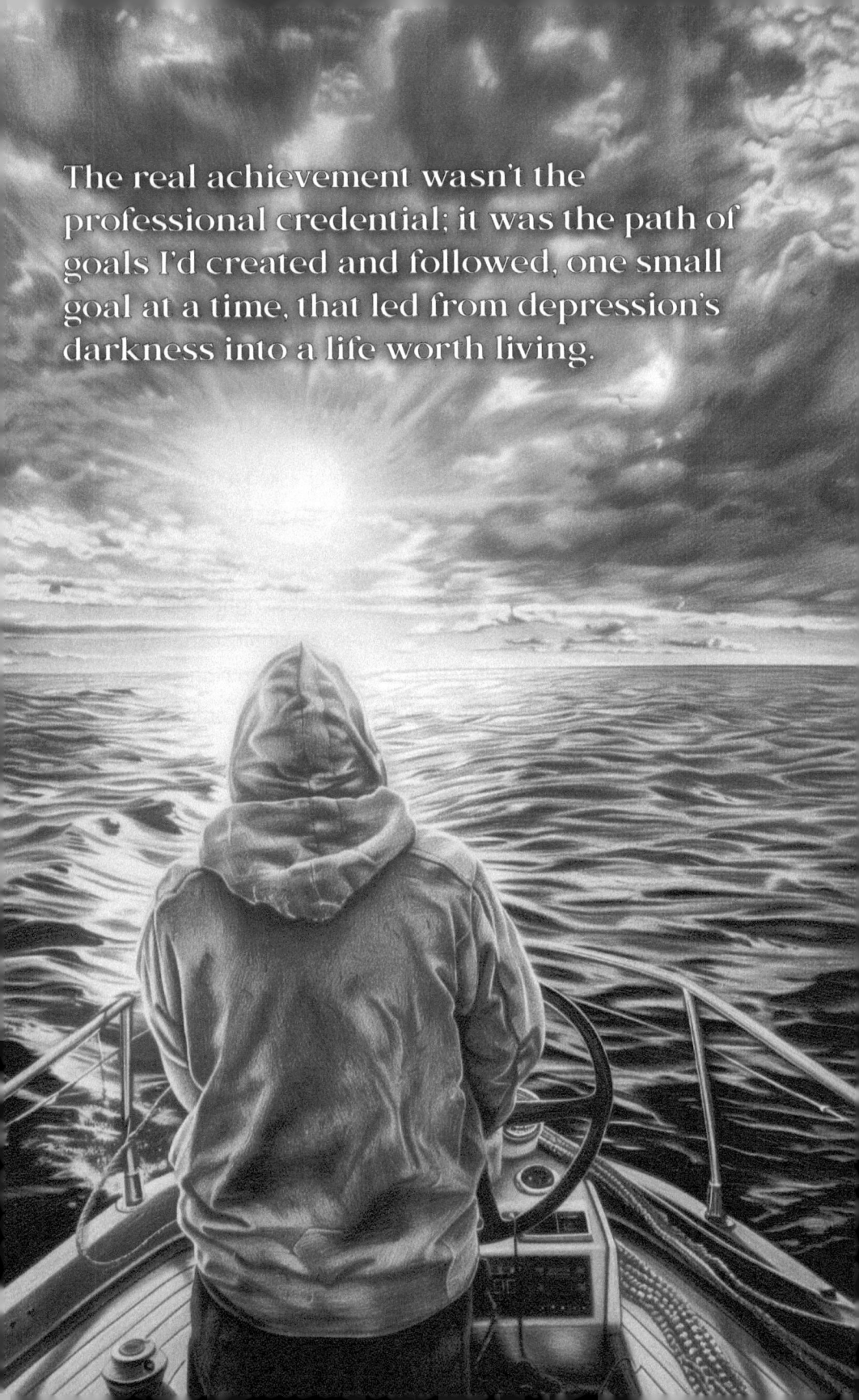

The real achievement wasn't the professional credential; it was the path of goals I'd created and followed, one small goal at a time, that led from depression's darkness into a life worth living.

For anyone caught in the overthinking trap, this approach offers both practical structure and gentle compassion. The small goals acknowledge your current limitations while creating concrete paths toward growth. They honor the reality that recovery isn't a single leap but a series of manageable steps: each one possible, each one moving you forward, each one quieting the noise a little more.

FINDING STRENGTH IN LIFE'S UNCERTAINTIES

The interview was going well until the partner asked a question I hadn't prepared for: "Where do you see yourself in ten years?"

Two years earlier, this question would have triggered an avalanche of anxiety. I would have scrambled to construct the "right" answer—some impressive career trajectory that showed ambition, certainty, and a master plan. The overthinking would have kicked into high gear, analyzing every possible response for how it might be perceived.

But on this day, sitting across from the accounting firm partner, something different happened. I smiled and spoke a truth I wouldn't have dared admit before:

"You know, I used to think I could map out my entire future. Then I lost my banking career, lost my sister, and had to completely rebuild my life. What I learned is that ten-year plans are mostly an illusion. What I can tell you is the direction I'm moving, toward work that uses my analytical strengths while allowing me to be present for my family. I can tell you the values guiding my decisions. But exactly where will I be? I've made peace with not knowing that anymore."

The noise in my head, the frantic need to control and predict everything, had finally quieted. In its place was something I hadn't expected to find through crisis: a comfort with uncertainty that felt like freedom.

When my life collapsed, I was forced to encounter uncertainty in ways that shattered my illusions of control and predictability. Those illusions had actually been part of what made me vulnerable to depression in the first place. My identity was built on being the guy who had everything figured out, who never failed, who controlled every variable.

While initially terrifying, this disruption ultimately created an opportunity to develop a more flexible psychological approach less dependent on controlling outcomes. By necessity, I had to learn to function amid uncertainty, a skill that built resilience far beyond my immediate crisis.

This shift involved recognizing uncertainty not as a threat but as a field of possibility, containing potential for growth, discovery, and renewal that would never have been available if I'd maintained my status quo. This reframing didn't minimize the suffering of my crisis but extracted value from inevitable discomfort.

I began to embrace change as a catalyst for growth, a redemptive approach to setbacks and disruptions. Periods of upheaval became accelerated growth opportunities precisely because they disrupted established patterns that might otherwise have remained unexamined for decades.

What I didn't know then was that neurologically, crisis events create temporary increases in neuroplasticity, the brain's adaptability and capacity for creating new neural connections. My brain was literally more capable of change during this difficult period than it had been during times of stability. This heightened neuroplasticity created optimal conditions for psychological transformation, which I was able to harness through therapy, learning, and intentional practice.

I came to understand that the discomfort accompanying change wasn't signaling danger but development, similar to how muscle growth requires the productive stress of resistance training. This growth-oriented perspective reduced my resistance to change processes that were often inevitable anyway, redirecting energy from fighting reality toward adapting creatively.

I remember reading about Max Hawkins, a former Google engineer who created algorithms to randomly determine his location, activities, and social connections after leaving his prestigious tech career. While his approach seemed extreme, something about his deliberate uncertainty-seeking struck a chord with me. Here was someone who had voluntarily stepped into the very uncertainty I'd been forced into and was finding expansion and authenticity through it.

While few would choose such radical randomness, his experience demonstrated how embracing rather than avoiding the unknown creates unique development opportunities. For me, recovering from depression following major life disruptions, Hawkins's example offered a valuable perspective: What initially appeared as unwelcome chaos was actually clearing space for a more authentic life aligned with deeper values.

I began practicing what I came to call "trusting the journey," maintaining direction without demanding certainty about exact outcomes. I held goals with determined flexibility while remaining responsive to emerging opportunities and challenges. This balance between intentional action and openness to unexpected development created progress toward meaningful aims while avoiding the rigidity that had previously made me vulnerable to depression when plans inevitably encountered obstacles.

Practically, this meant preparing thoroughly for job interviews while releasing attachment to specific outcomes. It meant creating study schedules for my CPA exams while being flexible about adjusting them when life intervened. It meant setting boundaries around family time while staying open to the unexpected moments of connection that couldn't be scheduled.

The most surprising discovery was how this approach actually quieted the overthinking that had plagued me. When I stopped demanding certainty from an inherently uncertain world, the mental gymnastics of trying to control everything through excessive analysis became unnecessary. My mind no longer needed to spin endlessly through every possibility because I'd made peace with not knowing exactly what would happen.

This isn't about passive acceptance or giving up on goals. It's about holding ambitions with open hands rather than clenched fists, moving purposefully in meaningful directions while remaining adaptable about the exact path. It's about recognizing that the tight grip of certainty actually constrains us, while the flexible strength of uncertainty allows for growth and discovery.

The partner's response to my honest answer about the ten-year plan surprised me. Rather than seeing uncertainty as weakness, he nodded with recognition. "That's probably the most authentic answer I've heard to that question," he said. "And given what accounting firms will face in the coming decade, adaptability might be more valuable than any specific plan."

Two weeks later, I received the job offer.

The noise in my head has never completely disappeared; the overthinking still visits sometimes. But its character has changed from frantic attempts to control the uncontrollable to curious exploration of possibilities. In finding strength through uncertainty rather than despite it, I discovered a resilience that no amount of planning could have provided.

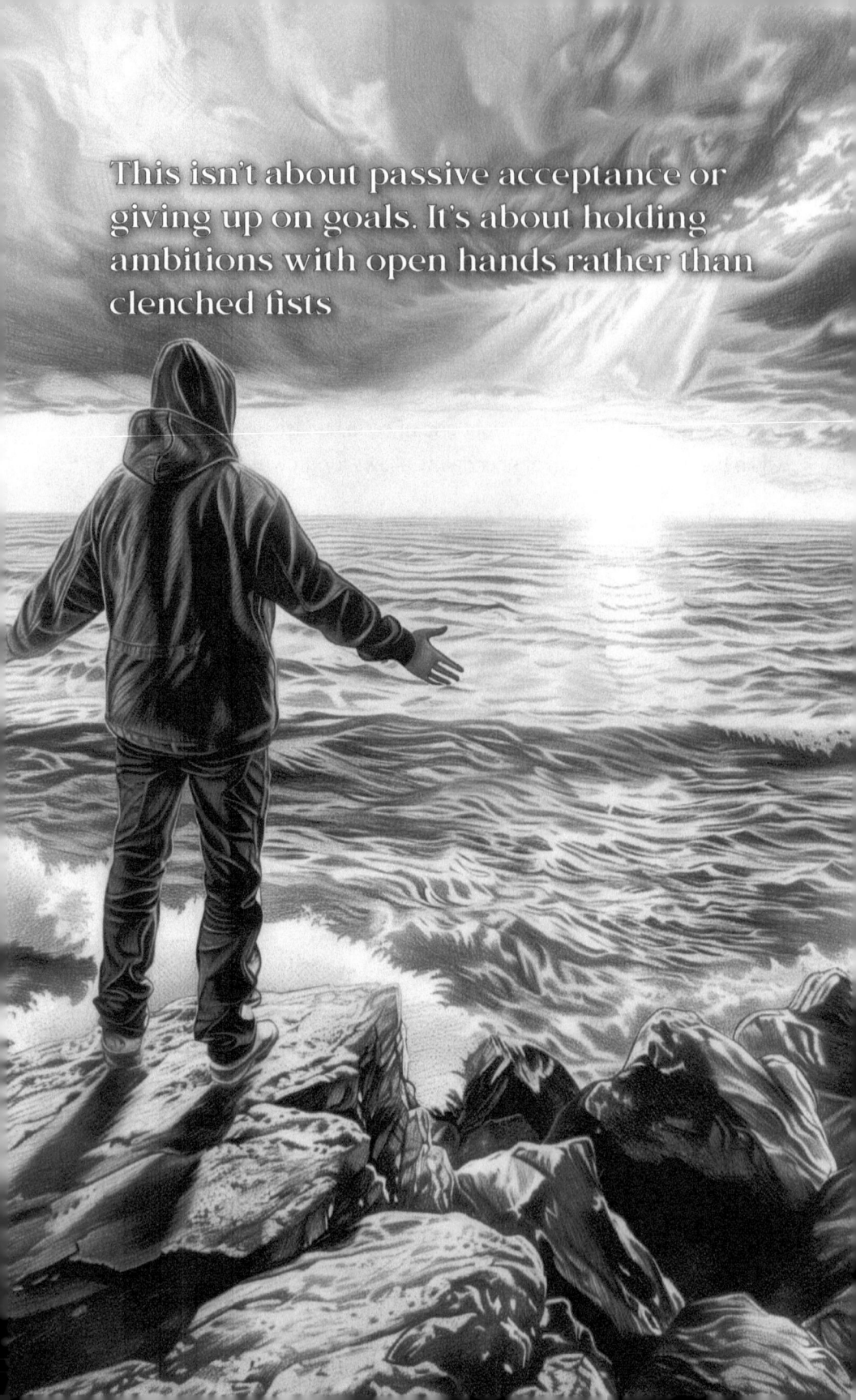

This isn't about passive acceptance or giving up on goals. It's about holding ambitions with open hands rather than clenched fists

Chapter 5:
Breaking the Silence—
The Power of Human Connection

Call it a clan, call it a network, call it a tribe,
call it a family: whatever you call it, whoever you are,
you need one.

–Jane Howard

Three months into my depression, I sat alone in my basement, surrounded by silence. I could hear the muffled sounds coming from upstairs of my wife and sons going about their evening routine. Friends had called and texted, but I'd stopped responding. My therapist's voice echoed in my head, "Isolation makes depression worse," but the thought of reaching out felt impossible. The noise in my head had convinced me of two contradictory things: that no one would understand what I was going through, and that burdening others with my struggles would only confirm my worthlessness.

The irony wasn't lost on me, even then. I was desperately lonely yet actively pushing away connection. I craved understanding but couldn't bear to be seen in my broken state. I needed support more than ever, yet found myself unable to accept it.

This painful contradiction is one that many men experience during depression and life crises. At precisely the moment when human connection becomes most vital to our healing, we retreat into isolation. The overthinking mind constructs elaborate justifications for this withdrawal: We're protecting others from our negativity, we're demonstrating strength through self-reliance, and we're avoiding rejection from those who wouldn't understand anyway.

What I didn't yet grasp was how central human connection would be to quieting that noise in my head. The path out of the overthinking trap isn't a solo journey. It can't be. Our brains are fundamentally social organs, shaped by and healed through relationships with others.

My breakthrough began with a simple text from a college friend: "I'm in town next week. No pressure to talk about anything serious, but I'd like to see you." Something about his no-pressure approach made it possible for me to say yes when I'd been saying no to everyone else. That coffee meeting—awkward at first, then increasingly comfortable—became the first thin thread reconnecting me to the world beyond my own suffering.

When Depression Whispers, "Stay Alone"

The first text I ignored was from my oldest friend, asking if I wanted to watch the game that weekend. The second was from my brother, checking in after not hearing from me for weeks. By the third month of my depression, I had stopped answering the phone entirely, letting calls go to voicemail that I never listened to. When my wife gently suggested having her parents over for dinner, I manufactured excuses until she stopped asking.

I told myself I was protecting others from my darkness. I convinced myself no one really wanted to be around me anyway. I believed I was giving everyone a break from my constant negativity. But beneath these justifications was a simpler truth: Depression was whispering, "Stay alone," and I was listening.

The basement became my refuge, or, more accurately, my hiding place. I'd make dinner, eat quickly with minimal conversation, then retreat downstairs with the excuse of "needing to decompress." Hours would pass as I stared at television shows I barely registered, my mind cycling through the same dark thoughts while physical distance reinforced my emotional isolation.

What I didn't understand then was how this isolation was not just a symptom of my depression but fuel for its fire. Each connection I severed strengthened depression's hold. Each invitation I declined confirmed the story in my head that I was broken beyond repair. Each day spent in self-imposed exile made the next day's loneliness feel more normal, more deserved.

Depression and isolation form a dangerous partnership, each intensifying the other through multiple reinforcing mechanisms. The social withdrawal that feels so natural during depression stems from several factors: the crushing fatigue that makes even simple conversations feel exhausting, heightened sensitivity to any hint of rejection or criticism, diminished ability to enjoy interactions that were once pleasurable, and deep shame about what you're experiencing.

Once this withdrawal begins, it accelerates depression by removing the essential social connections that would normally help regulate your mood. It eliminates opportunities for conversations that might challenge your negative perspective. It removes positive experiences that could counter the relentless negative thought patterns. And, perhaps most damagingly, it seems to confirm those depressive beliefs about being fundamentally disconnected and unworthy of connection.

Breaking this isolation cycle isn't just a nice add-on to depression recovery; it's absolutely crucial to finding your way back.

Breaking this isolation cycle isn't just a nice add-on to depression recovery; it's absolutely crucial to finding your way back.

As men, we face particular challenges in this area due to relationship patterns that many of us established long before depression arrived. Research consistently shows that men typically maintain fewer close confidants than women, engage less frequently in emotionally supportive conversations, and more commonly rely on romantic partners as their primary or sole emotional support (McKenzie et al., 2018).

I fit this pattern perfectly. Before depression hit, my wife was the only person who knew my inner emotional life. My friendships, while enjoyable, rarely ventured beyond shared activities and surface-level conversations. I hadn't practiced the skill of reaching out when struggling because I'd never really needed to—until suddenly I did and found myself without the tools or experience to know how to do so.

These patterns mean that when depression strikes, many of us lack established support networks capable of providing varied emotional resources. The masculine socialization most of us received framed seeking support as weakness rather than wisdom, creating additional barriers to connection precisely when it's most needed.

I remember the shame I felt the first time I broke down crying in my therapist's office. "I'm sorry," I kept saying, as though my tears were offensive or inappropriate. She gently pointed out that I was apologizing for being human. That observation struck me deeply. I had so internalized the message that men shouldn't need support that I was apologizing for having normal human emotions and needs.

The resulting isolation leaves many men attempting to overcome extreme psychological distress with minimal interpersonal resources. It's like trying to climb out of a pit with no rope, no ladder, and no helping hands—technically possible, perhaps, but unnecessarily difficult and far less likely to be successful.

What I didn't know during those months in the basement was how my isolation wasn't just making me feel worse emotionally; it was creating actual biological changes that reinforced my depression. Prolonged isolation correlates with increased inflammation in the body, disrupted stress hormone regulation, diminished immune function, and altered activity in brain regions associated with processing rewards and regulating emotions (Donovan et al., 2020).

These biological changes directly intensify depression symptoms while making treatments less effective. Social neuroscience research shows that social pain activates many of the same neural pathways as physical pain, making isolation not merely emotionally unpleasant but neurologically damaging (Zhang et al., 2020). This research explains why addressing isolation represents not an optional "feel-good" activity but an essential biological intervention in depression recovery.

My path out of isolation began small, with that coffee with my college friend I mentioned earlier. I remember how the simple act of sitting across from someone who knew me before depression, who could see beyond my current state, temporarily quieted the noise in my head. For a brief hour, the constant self-critical thoughts were interrupted by ordinary conversation about his job, my kids, and changes in our hometown.

I left that coffee shop slightly less convinced of depression's central lie, that I was fundamentally alone and disconnected from others. That tiny crack in depression's narrative was enough to make the next connection slightly easier, and the next one after that, and so on.

Breaking the isolation doesn't require grand social gestures or instantly rebuilding a full social calendar. It starts with a single text answered, a single invitation accepted, and a single honest conversation about how you're really doing. Each small step challenges depression's whisper to "stay alone" and reminds your brain and body of their fundamental need for human connection.

The noise in my head never fully quieted until I found my way back to others. Not despite my brokenness, but with it—visible, acknowledged, and still worthy of connection.

REACHING OUT: BUILDING YOUR CIRCLE OF SUPPORT

The first time I told someone outside my immediate family about my depression, my heart was pounding so hard I could barely hear myself speak. I'd invited an old colleague for coffee, someone I'd always respected but had never been particularly close to. After 20 minutes of small talk that felt like an eternity, I finally managed to say it:

"I've been going through a really rough time. Depression. It's why I left banking."

I braced myself for awkwardness, pity, or worst of all, some well-meaning but useless advice about positive thinking. Instead, he nodded, held my gaze, and said, "That took courage to share. Thank you for trusting me with that."

Something shifted in that moment. The constant noise in my head—the voice that insisted I should handle everything alone, that reaching out was weakness, that no one would understand—briefly quieted. In its place was a surprising feeling of relief. I hadn't realized how exhausting it had been to maintain the façade that everything was fine.

That conversation became the first intentional step in building what I now call my circle of support—the network of relationships that proved essential to my recovery and continues to sustain my mental health today.

What I didn't understand then was how that simple human connection was doing far more than providing momentary emotional comfort. It was actually changing my brain chemistry in ways that directly countered my depression.

Research shows that quality social connections reduce cortisol (the stress hormone that depression sends into overdrive), increase oxytocin (often called the "bonding hormone"), improve immune function, and activate reward pathways in the brain that fight depression's notorious ability to drain joy from everything (Trachtenberg, 2024). These biological effects explain why social support consistently emerges as one of the strongest predictors of positive mental health outcomes across diverse populations and conditions.

For men specifically, regular social connection correlates with reduced depression severity, faster recovery, and significantly lower suicide risk, even when controlling for other factors like income or relationship status. These benefits become particularly pronounced when our connections allow for authentic expression rather than the constant performance or impression management many of us habitually maintain.

Building these connections isn't easy, especially when depression has already isolated you. I faced numerous barriers, both practical and psychological, and you likely will, too.

My practical barriers included crushing work hours at my telemarketing job that left little energy for socializing, living in a different city from most of my old friends, and the loss of my banking colleagues who had formed most of my previous social network. Perhaps you're facing similar challenges—limited time, geographical distance from potential support, financial pressures, or social networks disrupted by life changes.

But honestly, the psychological barriers proved far more challenging: I was terrified of burdening others with my problems. I worried that admitting my struggle would make me appear weak or incompetent. I felt anxious about potential rejection if I showed my authentic self. I was uncertain about how much to share and with whom. And most pervasively, my depression-fueled belief that I was fundamentally unworthy of support made reaching out feel almost impossible.

I discovered, through both painful trials and unexpected successes, several strategies for overcoming these barriers. I started with limited, structured interactions that gradually increased in depth—coffee with clear start and end times, for example—before attempting deeper conversations. I sought connections based on shared activities rather than explicitly emotional exchanges, joining a weekend hiking group where conversation could flow naturally alongside movement. I utilized technology to maintain connections across distances, scheduling regular video calls with my brother, who lived across the country.

What proved most helpful was recognizing that different types of support serve complementary functions in recovery. The strongest support networks include professional, peer, and community connections, each offering something unique.

My therapist provided professional support: specialized knowledge, an objective perspective, and structured intervention within appropriate boundaries. She offered expertise I couldn't get elsewhere and maintained confidentiality that allowed me to be completely honest.

Peer support came through both individual friendships and, eventually, a men's support group I joined at my therapist's suggestion. These relationships offered mutual understanding based on shared experience. The first time another man in the group described thought patterns nearly identical to my own, the relief was palpable; I wasn't uniquely broken or alone in my struggle.

Community connection came through rejoining my neighborhood association and later volunteering at my son's school. These activities provided a broader social context, opportunities to contribute to something beyond myself, and identity dimensions beyond "depressed person" or "patient." When parents thanked me for organizing the school science fair, I briefly escaped the narrow self-definition depression had imposed.

The most resilient support networks incorporate elements of all three types, preventing over-reliance on any single relationship or support source. This diversity proved crucial when my therapist took maternity leave, when a close friend moved away, and when my support group temporarily disbanded. I wasn't left entirely without support during these transitions.

The hardest part of building this support circle was making those initial requests for help. I'd stare at my phone for an hour before sending a simple text asking to meet for coffee. I'd write and rewrite emails to old friends. I'd rehearse conversations endlessly, the overthinking machine in my head generating countless scenarios of rejection or burden.

What made these requests more manageable was starting with concrete, time-limited asks rather than open-ended emotional support. "Could we grab lunch Tuesday?" felt possible to ask when "I need your support during this difficult time" felt impossibly vulnerable. I learned to acknowledge the request's difficulty with simple phrases like, "I know you're busy, so I especially appreciate this." I offered reciprocity when possible: "I'd love to hear what's happening with you, too."

Perhaps most importantly, I gradually recognized that allowing others to help often benefited them as well. When I finally opened up to my brother about my struggles, he shared how helpless he had felt watching me withdraw. My willingness to accept his support gave him a way to convert that helpless concern into meaningful action.

The noise in my head didn't disappear immediately as I built these connections. But with each authentic exchange, each moment of being seen and accepted despite my struggles, the volume decreased. The constant internal chatter of self-criticism and catastrophizing had fewer uninterrupted hours to build momentum. Other voices—compassionate, reasonable, and encouraging—began to balance the harsh internal critic that depression had amplified to deafening levels.

Your circle of support won't look exactly like mine, but building it might be the most important step you take in quieting the overthinking that keeps you trapped in depression's grip. The connections you create become pathways out of isolation, bridges back to a world beyond your suffering.

How Helping Others Helps Yourself

Two years into my recovery, I found myself sitting across from Sally, the owner of a struggling bakery. She had stacks of disorganized receipts, tax notices she'd been afraid to open, and the desperate look of someone drowning in financial confusion. As a newly minted CPA, I'd started offering free monthly workshops at the community center on basic accounting for small business owners. Sally had approached me afterward, asking if I could look at her situation.

For the next two hours, I sorted through her paperwork, explained which notices were urgent, created a simple spreadsheet to track her cash flow, and outlined next steps. When we finished, she looked at me with tears in her eyes. "This is the first time I've felt hope in months," she said. "I've been so scared I was going to lose everything."

Driving home that evening, I realized something deep had shifted. For those two hours, the constant noise in my head—the rumination, self-doubt, and overanalysis that had been my companions for years—had gone completely silent. I'd been too absorbed in solving Sally's problems to listen to my own internal chaos. More surprisingly, the quiet persisted even after I left her bakery. The overthinking that usually filled my mind had been replaced by a simple sense of purpose and satisfaction.

I'd helped someone. It mattered. And in helping her, I'd somehow helped myself.

I'd helped someone. It mattered. And in helping her, I'd somehow helped myself.

This experience wasn't a one-off miracle. As I continued volunteering my accounting skills to struggling small businesses, I discovered a consistent pattern: The hours spent focused on others' problems provided reliable relief from my own mental noise. What started as a simple way to build my practice became something far more valuable: a pathway out of the overthinking trap.

Service to others provides a uniquely powerful restoration of purpose for many men recovering from depression and life crises. This approach works through multiple psychological mechanisms that directly counter depression's grip.

First, it focuses your attention outward rather than on internal distress. Depression thrives on self-focused rumination, the endless cycling through your own problems, flaws, and fears. Service breaks this cycle by directing attention toward others' needs, creating mental space where overthinking can't dominate.

Second, helping others provides concrete evidence of positive impact that directly challenges beliefs about worthlessness. When Sally thanked me for saving her business, depression couldn't simultaneously convince me I was useless. The tangible results of service create reality checks against depression's distorted narratives.

Third, service creates meaningful social roles and identities beyond "patient" or "sufferer." During my darkest times, my entire identity had shrunk to "depressed person." Through helping small business owners, I became "advisor," "problem-solver," and "community resource"—identities that expanded my sense of self beyond my struggles.

Finally, service activates neurological reward systems through prosocial behavior. Simply put, our brains are wired to feel good when we help others. Research consistently shows bidirectional benefits of service activities, with volunteers experiencing improved mood, reduced depression symptoms, and increased sense of meaning compared with control groups (Tse, 2018).

For men specifically, service activities offer a culturally acceptable context for developing emotional skills and connections that might otherwise feel uncomfortable or inaccessible. Discussing emotions directly often feels threatening to masculine identity for many of us, but sharing knowledge or skills to help someone feels natural and affirming.

My monthly workshops gradually expanded into a tight-knit community of local business owners who supported one another beyond accounting issues. This community identification provided essential belonging that counteracted the deep isolation and disconnection my depression had created. We evolved as social beings, neurologically designed for group participation, with belonging needs hardwired into our nervous systems. Finding communities with authentic values and interests creates not only social connection but also identity reinforcement and purpose clarification. My work with small businesses aligned perfectly with my values around financial education and local economic strength.

My community engagement started small, just a monthly two-hour workshop requiring minimal emotional exposure. This low-demand participation gradually increased as my capacity expanded. For others, initial involvement might include online communities requiring even less interaction, structured volunteer roles with clear expectations, or activity-based groups where conversation accompanies shared pursuits rather than serving as the primary focus.

As comfort and capacity increase, deeper engagement naturally develops through familiarity and trust-building. Within a year, I had formed genuine friendships with several business owners. The conversations that had once been strictly about balance sheets and tax strategies expanded to include life challenges, family stories, and eventually, when trust was established, my journey through depression.

Perhaps the most unexpected development was how these relationships evolved into mentorship, both receiving and providing guidance. Several experienced business owners took me under their wing as I established my accounting practice, offering advice on client relationships and business development. Simultaneously, I found myself mentoring newer entrepreneurs on financial fundamentals.

Serving as a mentor allowed me to share hard-earned wisdom while reinforcing my own learning and growth. Being mentored provided guidance from those who'd overcome similar challenges while creating accountability that supported my recovery actions. The structured nature of these mentoring relationships felt more accessible than open-ended emotional support, providing clear purpose and boundaries that reduced my discomfort with vulnerability.

This structure created a safe context for developing deeper connection skills that eventually transferred to other relationships in my life. The reciprocal nature of effective mentoring, where both participants recognize the exchange as mutually beneficial, reduced the stigma and shame I'd previously associated with "needing help."

Six months after our first meeting, Sally's bakery was thriving. She'd implemented the systems we created, caught up on tax obligations, and even hired an assistant. When she presented me with a cake at our group's year-end celebration, inscribed with "Thank you for saving Sweet Success Bakery," I felt a rush of emotion that momentarily threatened my carefully maintained composure.

"You didn't just help with my books," she said to the gathered group. "You helped me believe in myself again when I was ready to give up."

What she couldn't have known was how much she'd helped me, too. In focusing on her problems instead of my own, in using my skills to make a tangible difference, and in belonging to something larger than my individual struggle, I'd found my way to quiet the noise that had once seemed inescapable.

The path out of overthinking isn't just about looking inward; it's about reaching outward. When we help others, we help ourselves in ways no amount of self-focus ever could. The hand you extend to someone else just might be the one that pulls you free.

Healing Old Wounds, Rebuilding Trust

"I don't know who you are anymore," my wife said quietly one evening as I stared blankly at the television in our living room. "You're here, but you're not really here. I feel like I'm raising our kids alone."

Her words cut through the fog of my depression for just a moment, long enough to glimpse the damage my condition was causing to those I loved most. Then the fog closed in again, and I retreated to the basement, which had become my familiar escape.

That conversation happened six months into my depression, but it would be another three months before I could really hear what she was saying. When I finally began receiving treatment and slowly emerged from depression's grip, I faced a painful reality: My illness hadn't just hurt me. It had created wounds in my relationships that needed healing.

The recovery journey isn't just about fixing what's broken inside yourself; it's also about repairing the connections that depression has damaged along the way. For me, this meant rebuilding trust with my wife and learning how to be truly present for my kids again.

My first attempt at relationship repair was well-intentioned but flawed. Feeling guilty about how my depression had affected my family, I made grand promises about how everything would be different now. "I'll make it up to you," I assured my wife. "You'll see; I'll be better than before."

My therapist gently pointed out what I couldn't yet see: Trust isn't rebuilt through promises, no matter how sincere. It's rebuilt through consistent actions over time.

The healing process began with something surprisingly difficult—honest acknowledgment of how my condition had affected my loved ones. Not through beating myself up or excessive apologies, but through genuinely recognizing their experience during my depression.

"I know I wasn't really present for months," I told my wife during a quiet moment. "You carried everything—the household, parenting, and emotional support—while I was unable to contribute. That wasn't fair to you, and I understand why you felt alone. I'm not asking for forgiveness right now. I just want you to know that I see what you went through."

This acknowledgment validated her legitimate feelings without expectation of immediate forgiveness. It communicated respect for her experience rather than asking her to quickly move past it.

The real work—consistently demonstrating new patterns rather than just talking about them—came next. Small actions built upon one another: being fully present during family dinners instead of mentally checking out, taking our kids to the park on weekends to give my wife some time alone, and asking about her day and actually listening to the answer.

These weren't dramatic gestures. They were ordinary moments of connection that, strung together over months, gradually rebuilt what had been damaged. Some days I fell short, slipping into old patterns of withdrawal when stress hit. The difference was that now I could recognize when it happened and find my way back to presence more quickly.

I discovered that relationship healing, like personal recovery, occurs gradually rather than through single conversations or gestures. There were setbacks and awkward moments alongside the progress. Trust that had been damaged over months couldn't be repaired overnight, no matter how much I wished it could.

As my recovery continued, I recognized how my approach to relationships had always emphasized doing over being, problem-solving over presence, and activities over emotions. These traditional male patterns had value in certain contexts but created significant limitations in genuine connection, limitations that became painfully obvious during recovery.

Expanding my relationship capacities meant developing skills that hadn't come naturally to me: emotional disclosure beyond surface-level reports, truly listening without immediately trying to fix problems, expressing needs directly instead of expecting others to guess them, and tolerating the discomfort of vulnerability.

These weren't innate talents but skills I could develop through practice, improving with consistent effort despite initial awkwardness. My therapist provided specific exercises rather than vague suggestions to "open up more." We practiced actual conversations, reviewed interactions to identify missed connection opportunities, and established clear feedback mechanisms so I could learn what worked.

Interestingly, I found it easier to practice these skills in new relationships than in established ones. The men's support group provided a fresh context where I could experiment with more authentic communication without the weight of established patterns. My volunteer work with small business owners created opportunities to balance professional guidance with genuine human connection.

This made the recovery period an optimal time for establishing healthier connection habits that eventually transferred to my closest relationships. These new patterns balanced authenticity with appropriate boundaries, vulnerability with strength, and receiving support with giving it.

I noticed something powerful as these changes took hold: The constant noise in my head, the overthinking that had been my constant companion, began to quiet during genuine connections. When I was truly present with my wife, fully engaged with my kids, or deeply listening to a client's concerns, the mental chatter faded into the background. Real connection created a respite from rumination that no amount of solo effort had achieved.

A turning point came when my sister's two teenage children came to live with us temporarily during a difficult transition in their lives. Suddenly, I found myself in a godfather role to two adolescents struggling with their own challenges. Rather than seeing this as an additional burden during my recovery, I discovered it was actually a healing opportunity.

With these teens, I could practice the presence, listening, and emotional availability I'd been working to develop. I didn't have to be perfect; they didn't expect that. I just needed to be consistently there, genuinely interested in their lives, and honest about my journey.

When my nephew started struggling in school, we began meeting weekly to review his work. These sessions gradually evolved from homework help to deeper conversations about his frustrations, fears, and hopes. One evening, after working through a particularly challenging math assignment, he looked at me and said, "You know, you're the only adult who doesn't make me feel stupid when I don't understand something."

In that moment, the noise in my head went completely silent. I was fully present, connecting human to human, offering something I hadn't been able to give during my depression: my complete attention and acceptance.

Becoming a positive influence for others marked a significant recovery milestone. My capacity had expanded from merely receiving support to providing it. This transition occurred gradually, with periods of needing more intensive help interspersed with increasing ability to offer it to others. The balance shifted over time, creating a virtuous cycle where giving support strengthened my ability to maintain my own well-being.

The relationships in my life today bear little resemblance to those during my depression. The wounds haven't disappeared completely; there are still sensitive areas, and there are still moments when trust feels fragile. But the connections have deepened in ways I could never have imagined during those isolated months in the basement.

The noise of overthinking finally found its match in the quiet power of genuine human connection. In reaching out to others, in being reached, I found healing that no amount of solitary effort could have achieved.

CHAPTER 6:
REWRITING YOUR STORY— FINDING AUTHENTIC PURPOSE

Success is not final, failure is not fatal:
It is the courage to continue that counts.

–WINSTON CHURCHILL

Six months after receiving my CPA license, I found myself in a job interview at one of the city's largest accounting firms. The position offered prestige, a significant salary increase, and the kind of professional validation I'd been chasing most of my adult life. The interviewers were clearly impressed with my credentials and experience. An offer seemed certain.

As I sat there in my carefully pressed suit, nodding and smiling at all the right moments, a familiar noise started in my head—not the destructive rumination of depression this time, but a different kind of overthinking. A voice questioning whether this path was what I truly wanted.

The prestigious firm would mean 60-hour weeks during tax season. It would mean missing my kids' baseball games. It would mean returning to the high-pressure environment that had contributed to my breakdown years earlier.

I realized with sudden clarity that I was about to trade my hard-won recovery for a version of success that looked good on paper but violated everything I'd learned about what actually mattered to me.

Mid-interview, I did something that would have been unthinkable to my pre-depression self. I thanked the partners for their time and withdrew my application. The noise in my head didn't exactly stop in that moment, but it changed. Instead of anxious chatter, I felt a quiet certainty. I was choosing my own definition of success, not the one I'd inherited from others.

BEYOND THE PAYCHECK AND POSITION: WHAT REALLY MATTERS

The day, years earlier, when I received my vice president promotion at the bank, was supposed to be the pinnacle of success, the moment I'd been working toward since college. At age 32, I had the corner office, the salary, the respect of my colleagues, and the validation of my superiors. On paper, I had "made it."

That evening, my wife organized a small celebration dinner. Friends toasted my achievement. My parents called to express their pride. Everyone seemed genuinely happy for me—everyone except, strangely, myself.

Alone in our bathroom later that night, I stared at my reflection and felt a disturbing emptiness. The triumph I'd anticipated, the satisfaction I'd expected, the sense of arrival I'd been promised—none of it materialized. Instead, I felt a vague hollowness and the immediate pressure to start working toward the next promotion. The finish line I'd crossed simply revealed another, longer race ahead.

I didn't know it then, but this emptiness was the first whisper of the depression that would eventually engulf me. It was also my first encounter with what psychologists call the "arrival fallacy," the discovery that achieving long-pursued goals often fails to provide the fulfillment we expect.

The traditional markers of success—the wealth I was accumulating, my career advancement, the status I'd acquired, the house and car I'd purchased—had organized my entire adult life. I'd never questioned whether these were the right metrics for a successful life. They were simply the measures everyone around me used, the benchmarks my father had pursued, the standards celebrated in every business magazine and family gathering.

What I didn't understand until my breakdown forced me to reconsider everything was how these external validation sources remain inherently unstable. They're subject to market fluctuations, organizational changes, and inevitable comparisons with others who have more. Building my identity on these shifting foundations had created a persistent insecurity that no achievement could resolve.

The promotion that should have satisfied me only heightened my anxiety about maintaining my position and pursuing the next level. The salary increase immediately adjusted my lifestyle upward, creating new financial pressures rather than security. The status recognition quickly faded, requiring constant renewal through new achievements.

I had stepped onto an achievement treadmill that constantly accelerated but never reached a destination. No wonder the noise in my head—the constant analysis, comparison, and self-assessment—never quieted. The metrics I was using guaranteed perpetual insecurity.

When my career collapsed following my sister's death and subsequent depression, these external metrics collapsed simultaneously, removing multiple identity pillars without established alternatives. Who was I without my vice president title? What was my worth without my salary? How did I measure my days without targets and bonuses?

Recovery necessitated a fundamental reassessment of the success definitions that had previously organized my life. This wasn't an optional philosophical exercise; it was survival. I needed new metrics that wouldn't crumble with the next market downturn or corporate restructuring.

The emptiness I'd felt even at the height of my achievement now made perfect sense. I had been pursuing externally defined success disconnected from my intrinsic values, creating achievement without meaning. The culturally reinforced expectation that such achievements should produce happiness created additional distress when this anticipated emotional payoff failed to materialize.

My therapist asked a question that started shifting my perspective: "When was the last time you lost track of time because you were so engaged in what you were doing?"

I had to think hard. It wasn't during boardroom presentations or client negotiations, despite my skill at these activities. It was helping my nephew understand his math homework. It was organizing financial workshops for the community center. It was the rare weekend when I set work aside and was fully present with my family.

This simple question began the process of creating personalized success definitions aligned with my intrinsic values rather than external expectations or comparative measures. I started examining which activities and experiences created genuine engagement and meaning regardless of recognition or reward.

Gradually, I developed new metrics for measuring my days: How present was I with the people I love? Did I use my skills to help someone today? Did I maintain my boundaries and honor my health? Did I learn something new? Did I experience moments of joy or peace?

These new metrics shared important characteristics that my old ones lacked. They measured process quality rather than solely outcomes—how I lived each day rather than simply what I accomplished. They remained largely within my control rather than dependent on others' evaluations or market conditions. They aligned with my authentic interests rather than imposed expectations. And they connected daily actions with larger values like connection, growth, contribution, and well-being.

This approach shifted my focus from accumulating achievements toward experiencing life quality, from having toward being. The noise in my head began to quiet as I stopped constantly measuring myself against external yardsticks that were constantly moving and impossible to achieve.

At my small accounting practice today, I make significantly less money than I did as a banking vice president. My car is older, my house is more modest, and my title is less impressive at cocktail parties. By my old metrics, I've taken several steps backward.

Yet the constant noise of overthinking that plagued me even at the height of my "success" has largely subsided. When I help a small business owner understand their finances, when I make it home for dinner with my family, and when I have energy left for things that bring me joy, I experience a solid sense of rightness that no promotion ever provided.

UNCOVERING YOUR INNER COMPASS

"Why accounting?" my therapist asked during our session, six months into my recovery. "Of all the directions you could go after banking, why that path?"

The question caught me off guard. I'd been so focused on the practical aspects of my career change—stability, employability, structured path forward—that I hadn't deeply examined what drew me to this specific field.

"I'm good with numbers," I said, offering the simplest explanation. "And the job market is stable."

She nodded, then asked something that would prove life-changing: "When you're working with financial information, what moments feel most meaningful to you?"

I closed my eyes and really considered this. The answer surprised me.

"It's when I'm helping someone understand something that was confusing them. When I take financial chaos and create order that they can use to make decisions. When they go from feeling overwhelmed to feeling in control." I opened my eyes. "It's not actually about the numbers. It's about using the numbers to create clarity for people who are lost in the confusion."

Something shifted in that moment. The noise in my head—the constant questioning of my new direction, the worry about starting over, the comparison with my former status—suddenly quieted. I'd stumbled upon something that felt undeniably true, a value so authentically mine that it silenced the overthinking.

Creating clarity from confusion. This wasn't a value I'd inherited from my achievement-oriented father or absorbed from my status-conscious banking colleagues. It was something genuinely mine, something that had always brought me satisfaction across different contexts—from helping my nephew with math to organizing community workshops to my new accounting studies.

This was my first experience with what I now call my "inner compass," the set of core values that point toward what truly matters to me beneath the noise of shoulds, expectations, and habits.

Identifying these core values after a crisis provides an essential foundation for rebuilding a meaningful life aligned with authentic priorities rather than external expectations or patterns you've fallen into. This process involves distinguishing between inherited values absorbed from family, culture, or profession and deeply personal values reflecting your authentic nature and experiences.

My therapist guided me through several approaches to uncover these core values. She asked me to examine peak positive experiences in my life for common elements. We explored when I'd felt most alive or engaged, regardless of whether those moments were "important" by conventional standards. We discussed what consistently generated anger or injustice reactions in me, recognizing that these strong emotional responses often signal violated values. And in an exercise that initially felt morbid but proved powerful, she asked what principles I would want mentioned in my eulogy—not accomplishments, but qualities and values.

What emerged surprised me with its consistency. Across diverse experiences, from professional achievements to personal relationships to hobbies, the same themes appeared repeatedly: creating order from chaos, providing clarity where there was confusion, building bridges of understanding, maintaining integrity even when costly, and creating security for those who depend on me.

These values provided coherent direction amid the uncertainty of my life transition. They became my inner compass when external markers of success had fallen away.

With this compass, I began connecting my emerging accounting career with personal meaning in ways I hadn't considered. What had started as a practical choice for stability transformed into a vocation that was consistent with my authentic values and strengths.

This alignment didn't require a dramatic additional career change—I was already on a new path that could embody my values—but it did change how I approached that path. Rather than seeing accounting merely as a technical profession focused on numbers and regulations, I recognized it as a way to create clarity from financial confusion, to build bridges of understanding between numbers and decisions, and to establish order that created security.

This reframing shifted my relationship with identical activities from obligation to expression, from potentially depleting to energizing. The same tax form I might have approached mechanically became an opportunity to create clarity for a client overwhelmed by financial complexity.

My experience with depression and financial upheaval, painful as it was, uniquely equipped me to serve others facing similar challenges. I understood the emotional weight of financial confusion in a way my previous banking self never could. I knew what it meant to feel overwhelmed by paperwork that represented security and the future.

This perspective is consistent with what psychiatrist Viktor Frankl observed after surviving concentration camps: Meaning emerges not from what life offers us but from what we offer life through our unique combination of experiences, talents, and perspectives (Frankl, 2018). My suffering wasn't meaningless if it gave me the tools to help others through similar terrain.

Several practical exercises helped me further refine this purpose. I identified the intersection between my personal strengths (analytical thinking, communication, and systematic organization), my meaningful experiences (including depression and financial crisis), and world needs (financial clarity, especially for those in difficult transitions). I paid attention to activities that created flow states where time seemed to disappear, often explaining complex financial concepts in accessible ways. And I noticed what issues consistently captured my attention and emotional energy—in particular, how financial stress affected mental health and family stability.

My suffering wasn't meaningless if it gave me the tools to help others through similar terrain.

THE COURAGE TO SILENCE YOUR INNER CRITIC

The email inviting me to speak at the Small Business Association's annual conference sat in my inbox for three days before I could bring myself to respond. As the founder of a growing accounting practice specializing in business transitions, I was objectively qualified. My client list was strong. My reputation was solid.

Yet the voice in my head wouldn't stop:

Who are you to present yourself as an expert? You had a mental break-down. You lost your banking career. You're a second-career accountant who barely survived his own financial crisis. If they knew your history, they'd never have invited you.

This wasn't ordinary nervousness about public speaking. It was impostor syndrome, the persistent fear of being exposed as inadequate despite clear evidence of competence. And it was shouting so loudly I could barely hear myself think.

The night before the response deadline, I sat at my kitchen table after everyone had gone to bed. My finger hovered over the "decline with regrets" template I'd drafted. Then I noticed the small box on the shelf above my laptop, the one where I kept what my therapist had suggested I create years earlier: an evidence journal.

I opened it and began reading through the notes and emails I'd collected. Client testimonials describing how I'd helped them understand their finances for the first time. Thank you cards from small business owners who'd weath-ered difficult transitions with my guidance. Feedback from workshop partic-ipants who appreciated my straightforward explanations of complex topics.

The noise in my head didn't disappear completely, but it softened enough for me to close the decline email, open a fresh draft, and type, "I would be honored to speak at your conference."

Men who have experienced significant failure or setbacks frequently develop impostor syndrome, like I did. This goes beyond typical self-doubt; it's a persistent conviction that any success is accidental and eventual exposure as a fraud is inevitable.

This phenomenon stems from several sources that might feel painfully familiar. There's the internalized shame about past difficulties—my break-down, my career collapse, and my period of unemployment. There's the disrupted self-trust that follows unexpected failures—if I didn't see the breakdown coming, how can I trust my judgment now? There's a new hyperawareness of limitations revealed through crisis—the vulnerabilities and weaknesses I can no longer pretend don't exist. And there's the con-stant fear that others will discover my "damaged" history and reevaluate everything they thought about me.

For those of us recovering from depression or public setbacks, this impos-tor experience often feels more intense than typical performance anxi-ety. It carries existential weight connected to rebuilding our very iden-tity. The resulting self-doubt creates particular challenges during career rebuilding or new endeavors, as internal criticism constantly undermines efforts and amplifies normal learning challenges into perceived evidence of fundamental inadequacy.

When I made a minor calculation error in a client presentation, the inner critic didn't say, *You made a mistake*. It said, *You see? This proves you don't belong in this profession. A real accountant wouldn't make that error.*

Through therapy and practice, I gradually developed strategies for build-ing authentic confidence—not the façade of certainty I'd maintained in my banking days, but something more genuine and ultimately more durable.

The first important insight was distinguishing between confidence and certainty. True confidence isn't about being certain nothing will go wrong but about trusting your ability to handle challenges regardless of the outcome. This distinction shifted my focus from the impossible goal of avoiding all failure toward developing resilience that would serve me regardless of results.

Several practical approaches helped quiet my inner critic. The evidence journal I mentioned earlier became crucial, a concrete collection of competence demonstrations that countered my distorted self-perception. When the noise in my head insisted I was a fraud, these tangible reminders of impact and ability provided a reality check.

I practiced self-compassion by treating myself with the same kindness I would offer a friend rather than the harsh criticism I habitually directed inward. When I made that calculation error, I learned to say to myself, *Everyone makes mistakes occasionally. This doesn't define your ability*, rather than, *This proves you're inadequate*.

I utilized "as if" techniques during particularly challenging situations, temporarily acting like I felt confident even when I didn't. Before client presentations, I would stand in postures associated with confidence, speak at a pace suggesting comfort, and make the eye contact a confident person would make. Remarkably, these external behaviors often created internal shifts, generating positive feedback cycles that built genuine confidence.

Perhaps most importantly, I developed realistic assessments of both strengths and limitations to replace global negative self-evaluations. Instead of *I'm a fraud who doesn't belong here*, I learned to think, *I have strong skills in explaining financial concepts clearly and building client trust. I'm still developing expertise in tax law for certain industries*. This accurate self-knowledge provided a foundation far more stable than either blanket self-criticism or inflated self-assurance.

The real breakthrough came when I began embracing my experience as a source of wisdom rather than as a liability to hide. My experience with depression, career collapse, and rebuilding gave me insights and capacities unavailable to those who had followed smoother paths. My ability to deal with uncertainty, rebuild after collapse, manage difficult emotions, and maintain perspective during challenges represented wisdom increasingly valued in both business and personal contexts.

During that Small Business Association presentation, I did something I hadn't planned. In discussing financial transitions, I briefly mentioned my career change following a personal crisis. I didn't detail my depression or breakdown, but I acknowledged that my expertise came partly from personal experience with major life transitions.

After the talk, several attendees approached specifically because of that moment of vulnerability. "I'm going through something similar," one woman confided. "Hearing that you rebuilt successfully gives me hope."

That day, the noise of the inner critic finally quieted—not because I had achieved perfection or certainty, but because I had integrated my full journey into my professional identity. What I had perceived as my greatest liability had become a unique asset. The very experiences my impostor syndrome had insisted I hide had become the source of my most valuable insights.

Speaking Your Truth: Finding Your Voice Again

The first time I tried to tell my story in the men's support group, no words came out. I sat there, mouth open, completely frozen as five men waited patiently. The therapist leading the group nodded with encouragement, but my voice had simply vanished. After an excruciating minute of silence, I managed to whisper, "I can't," and the group moved on to someone else.

That moment of failed speech was its own kind of rock bottom. Depression hadn't just taken my career, my confidence, and my sense of self; it had stolen my voice. The ability to articulate my experience and to speak my truth had disappeared under the weight of shame and fear.

For three months, I attended that weekly group in nearly complete silence. I'd occasionally answer direct questions with minimal responses but otherwise remained mute. The noise in my head was deafening: constant analysis about what others might think if they knew my full story, endless rehearsal of potential responses to imagined judgments, and obsessive concern about saying the "wrong" thing. This internal cacophony effectively drowned out my voice.

My journey back to speech began not with talking but with writing. My therapist suggested keeping a journal where no one but me would see my words. "Write what you can't yet say," she advised. "Your voice is still there. It just needs a safer place to emerge first."

Those early journal entries were messy, disjointed, and raw. I wrote about the shame of my breakdown, the grief over my sister's death, and the failure of my banking career. I wrote things I couldn't imagine ever saying aloud to another person. But in that private space, my voice began to strengthen.

After weeks of daily writing, I felt ready for a small step. During a one-on-one therapy session, I read aloud from my journal, not maintaining eye contact, hands shaking, but speaking the words nonetheless. My therapist listened without judgment, creating a space where my vulnerability felt held rather than exposed.

Finding the courage to share my story represented a crucial milestone in my recovery, turning private healing into something that could potentially help others. This courage developed gradually through progressive vulnerability with expanding audiences, moving from private journal writing to therapy disclosures to trusted individuals to wider sharing as my readiness increased.

Next came sharing with my wife not the sanitized version of my experience I'd been offering, but the messy truth, including the darkest thoughts I'd had. Her response—tears, embrace, and "thank you for trusting me with this"—gave me the courage to continue.

Six months after that initial frozen moment in the group, I finally spoke my full story aloud to those same men. My voice shook at first, but steadied as I continued. I shared not just what had happened to me, but what it had meant, how it had changed me, and what I was learning through recovery. When I finished, the silence held a different quality than before—not the emptiness of words trapped inside but the fullness of having been truly heard.

This progression honored both the value of authentic expression and my legitimate need for psychological safety during vulnerability. The decision to share more publicly involved thoughtful consideration of timing, boundaries around private details, and clarity about why I was sharing. I learned that effective story sharing focuses not on detailed trauma recounting but on meaningful narrative addressing struggle, turning points, insights gained, and the ongoing journey, emphasizing transformation rather than victimization.

Eventually, I found myself speaking at a community mental health awareness event, something I couldn't have imagined during those silent months. I didn't share every detail of my experience, maintaining appropriate boundaries around my most private struggles, but I offered enough authentic truth to potentially help someone else feeling isolated in similar darkness.

The healing power of self-expression extended beyond just telling my story. I discovered diverse forms of authentic communication and creative expression that continued to quiet the overthinking in my head.

Your journey back to speech might follow a different path than mine. You might find your voice through art, music, writing, or conversations with trusted others before you're ready for wider sharing. You might never choose to speak publicly about your experience, and that's completely okay.

What matters isn't how widely you share your story, but that you find ways to express your truth that feel authentic and healing to you. The voice that depression tried to silence contains wisdom, strength, and healing—not just for yourself, but potentially for others walking similar paths. When you're ready, in whatever form feels right, speaking your truth becomes one of the most powerful ways to finally quiet the noise.

The voice that depression tried to silence
contains wisdom, strength, and healing—not just for yourself, but potentially
for others walking similar paths

Chapter 7:
The Continuing Journey—
Nurturing Long-Term Well-Being

The secret of change is to focus all of your energy,
not on fighting the old, but on building the new.

–Socrates

Seven years after my deepest depression, I found myself sitting in my car in the office parking lot, unable to make myself go inside. The familiar heaviness had returned over the past few weeks—not as severe as before, but recognizable. Sleep had become restless again. Client calls felt increasingly draining. The noise in my head—that constant overthinking I thought I'd conquered—had been gradually increasing in volume.

My first thought was one of pure panic: *It's happening again. All that work, all that recovery, and I'm right back where I started.*

But then I noticed something different this time. I actually recognized what was happening. Instead of being blindsided by depression as I had been years earlier, I was aware of the subtle shifts in my mental landscape. And, more importantly, I knew what to do about them.

I called my therapist, whom I hadn't seen in over a year, and scheduled a session. I told my wife what I was experiencing instead of hiding it. I adjusted my client load temporarily. I returned to the daily walks that had gradually fallen off my schedule. Within three weeks, the heaviness lifted, and the mental noise quieted back to its manageable background hum.

This wasn't a failure of recovery. It was recovery working exactly as it should—not by preventing all future struggles, but by making sure I had the tools to respond effectively when they appeared.

This chapter addresses one of the most challenging aspects of mental health recovery: maintaining progress and preventing relapse. For many of us who have overcome depression, anxiety, or life crises, the fear of sliding back into darkness can be overwhelming. That fear itself can become a source of constant overthinking, creating the very mental noise we've worked so hard to quiet.

What I've learned through both personal experience and working with others is that sustainable recovery isn't about achieving some perfect state of permanent wellness. It's about developing the awareness, tools, and support systems that allow you to navigate the inevitable ups and downs of life without losing your way completely.

UNDERSTANDING RELAPSE IN MENTAL HEALTH

The moment I realized I was sliding back toward depression came on an ordinary Tuesday morning. My alarm went off, and instead of getting up, I hit snooze four times. When I finally dragged myself to the shower, I stood under the water for twenty minutes, lost in a fog of negative thoughts. At breakfast, I snapped at my son over a spilled glass of orange juice, then felt a wave of shame disproportionate to the minor incident.

None of these things alone meant much. But together, they formed a pattern I'd learned to recognize, the early warning signs that the noise in my head was starting to amplify again.

What I've come to understand, both through personal experience and conversations with other men who've gone through similar experiences, is that depression and anxiety are often recurring conditions, not unlike chronic physical illnesses that require ongoing management. They're not enemies you defeat once and for all, but companions you learn to manage over a lifetime.

I fell into this trap after my first successful treatment. Six months of therapy, lifestyle changes, and medication had lifted the heaviest depression. Feeling better, I gradually dropped all three—stopped therapy because I felt "fixed," abandoned my morning walks because work got busy, and decided with my doctor to taper off medication. Within four months, I was sliding back into the darkness, the overthinking noise growing louder each week.

What I've learned since is that recognizing your personal relapse triggers is essential for long-term wellness. These triggers often include work stress, relationship conflicts, financial pressure, health issues, significant life transitions, or anniversary reactions to past traumas.

For me, the perfect storm is work deadlines combined with disrupted sleep and skipped exercise. For my friend Mark, it's a conflict with his ex-wife over co-parenting arrangements. For another friend in my support group, it's financial uncertainty that reliably kicks his anxiety into overdrive. Your triggers will be specific to you, shaped by your history, biology, and circumstances.

The most effective approach to preventing relapse is developing an early warning system. This involves documenting your personal patterns: What specific changes in sleep, appetite, energy, socialization, thinking patterns, or behaviors typically precede your depression or anxiety? Creating a written inventory of these signs allows you to recognize them in their earliest stages, when intervention is most effective.

My therapist helped me create what she called a "personal dashboard," a checklist of my specific warning signs that I review weekly. They include sleeping past my alarm, skipping more than two planned workouts, checking email after 9 p.m., declining social invitations, and what my wife calls "the silent retreat," where I physically withdraw to my home office for hours.

Some men find a simple rating scale helpful, scoring their mental health daily from 1 to 10 and noting when scores begin trending downward. Others use technology; apps like MoodMission, Daylio, or Woebot can help track patterns and provide immediate coping strategies when needed.

Whatever system you develop, the goal is the same: to catch the slide before you're at the bottom of the hill. The noise of overthinking doesn't usually go from whisper to shout overnight; it increases gradually, giving you an opportunity to intervene—but only if you're paying attention.

After several years of practice, I can usually catch the downward trend within days rather than weeks. The moment I notice two or more warning signs persisting for more than a couple of days, I implement my "maintenance plan"—scheduled daily walks regardless of workload, at least one social connection, earlier bedtimes, a therapy check-in, and temporary work adjustments.

Understanding relapse doesn't mean living in fear of it. Paradoxically, acknowledging the possibility of future struggles actually reduces anxiety about them. When you know what to watch for and have a plan for responding, the prospect of occasional setbacks becomes manageable rather than terrifying.

The noise of overthinking doesn't usually go from whisper to shout overnight; it increases gradually, giving you an opportunity to intervene—but only if you're paying attention.

The noise might return from time to time, but it no longer has the power to define your life or your future. You've learned its language, recognized its early whispers, and developed the tools to quiet it once again.

DAILY RITUALS FOR MENTAL STRENGTH

Three years into my recovery, I found myself standing in my driveway at 5:30 a.m. in the pouring rain, debating whether to skip my morning walk. I had a major client presentation that afternoon. The weather was miserable. My bed was still warm.

Every reasonable excuse lined up in my mind. Yet something deeper in me knew the truth: This wasn't just about a walk. This daily ritual had become an essential anchor for my mental well-being. Skipping it when I felt good was one thing. Skipping it when stress was high was playing with fire.

I grabbed my rain jacket, put on my headphones, and stepped out into the downpour. Thirty minutes later, soaked but clear-headed, I felt the familiar quieting of the mental noise that had threatened to dominate my day. The presentation would still be challenging, but the constant overthinking had settled to a manageable hum.

That morning reinforced what experience had already taught me: Consistent self-care forms the foundation of relapse prevention. Yet, like many men, I've struggled to prioritize these practices amid work and family responsibilities. The old programming runs deep: Put work first, push through discomfort, and handle everything yourself.

What I've learned, sometimes the hard way, is that effective self-care isn't about occasional indulgence but rather daily habits that support mental wellness. It's not a luxury; it's maintenance as essential as changing your car's oil or paying your mortgage.

I started by identifying three non-negotiable practices that make a noticeable difference in my mood and energy: a 30-minute morning walk, 10 minutes of midday breathing exercises, and completely unplugging from work after dinner. These became appointments with myself that I kept with the same commitment I give to important client meetings or my kids' baseball games.

Your non-negotiables will be unique to you. Maybe it's 20 minutes of morning exercise, midday meditation, evening journaling, or a scheduled time for woodworking, music, or another hobby that absorbs your attention. The specific activities matter less than their regularity and their effectiveness in quieting your particular mental noise.

Among the most powerful practices I've found are mindfulness techniques. I initially resisted these as too "new age" for my practical mindset. But the evidence eventually convinced me to try a simple breathing practice using a straightforward app designed specifically for skeptical beginners like me.

Research shows that regular mindfulness meditation actually changes brain structure in regions associated with emotional regulation, self-awareness, and attention, all critical factors in maintaining mental health (Powell, 2018). The practice doesn't need to be complicated; even five minutes daily of focused breathing can build the "mental muscle" that helps you recognize unhelpful thought patterns before they spiral.

My daily practice is embarrassingly simple: ten minutes of following my breath while sitting in my car before entering the office. Nothing mystical or complicated. Yet this brief daily ritual has dramatically improved my ability to notice when overthinking starts to accelerate, allowing me to intervene before the noise becomes overwhelming.

Apps like Headspace offer specific programs for men, with straightforward approaches and minimal jargon. I found their "Basics" course and then their "Stress" pack particularly helpful in developing a sustainable practice.

I've also discovered that physical wellness directly impacts my mental health, creating either a protective buffer or increasing vulnerability to relapse. Regular exercise increases something called brain-derived neurotrophic factor (BDNF), essentially fertilizer for brain cells that supports mood regulation (Sleiman et al., 2016). Those morning walks aren't just clearing my head; they're literally nourishing my brain.

Quality sleep enables emotional processing and stress recovery, while nutrition affects neurotransmitter production and brain inflammation. Rather than approaching these areas with an all-or-nothing mindset, I focus on consistency over perfection. I won't always get eight hours of sleep, but I can maintain a consistent bedtime most nights. I won't eat perfectly, but I can ensure regular meals that include plenty of vegetables and protein.

I came to recognize these daily rituals not as burdens but as freedom, and that made all the difference. Each morning walk creates space between me and the noise in my head. Each breathing session reduces the grip of stress. Each good night's sleep strengthens my resilience for the next day's challenges.

BECOMING THE HERO OF YOUR STORY

Two years into my recovery, I sat in a new psychiatrist's office, listening as she recommended a medication I'd tried previously with significant side effects. When she paused, I hesitated, feeling the familiar pressure to simply nod and comply. Instead, I took a deep breath and said, "I appreciate the recommendation, but that particular medication caused serious problems for me before. Could we discuss alternatives that might work better with my history?"

She looked up from her notes, smiled, and replied, "Thank you for telling me that. Let's look at some other options that might be a better fit."

That simple exchange represented a huge shift in my approach to my mental health. The noise in my head—the overthinking about appearing difficult, questioning a professional's judgment, or seeming like a "problem patient"—momentarily flared but didn't override my ability to advocate for myself. I had stepped into the role of active participant rather than passive recipient in my care.

Taking responsibility for your mental health means shifting from a passive to an active role in your ongoing wellness. This doesn't mean handling everything alone—quite the opposite. It means becoming the primary coordinator of your support team, the central player rather than a spectator in your recovery story.

I started this shift by educating myself about depression and anxiety through reputable sources like the National Institute of Mental Health and major mental health organizations—not to self-diagnose or replace professional guidance, but to become an informed participant in conversations about my care. Understanding the basics of how different treatments work, typical timelines for improvement, and common challenges helped quiet the overthinking that thrived in uncertainty.

Next, I created what my therapist called a "personal mental health history," documenting which approaches had helped me in the past and which hadn't. This included medications, therapy techniques, lifestyle changes, and coping strategies, along with notes about their effectiveness and any side effects or challenges. This document became a personalized reference guide I could share with new providers or consult during difficult periods when my decision-making might be compromised.

Developing effective partnerships with mental health professionals significantly improved my long-term outcomes. Rather than viewing my

Taking responsibility for your mental health means shifting from a passive to an active role in your ongoing wellness

psychiatrist and therapist as authorities to be obeyed, I began approaching these relationships as collaborative partnerships. I came to appointments prepared with specific questions, tracked my response to treatments in a simple journal, and learned to speak up when something wasn't working.

I wasn't always comfortable with this at first. Like many men, I'd been socialized to remain passive in healthcare settings, reluctant to question recommendations or report when treatments weren't effective. The overthinking would kick in: *Who am I to question someone with a medical degree? Maybe I should just try harder to make this work.*

What finally silenced that noise was realizing that even the best mental health professionals can't read minds. My psychiatrist didn't know that medication caused insomnia unless I reported it. My therapist couldn't tell which techniques worked unless I provided feedback. My active participation wasn't challenging their expertise; it was providing essential information they needed to apply that expertise effectively.

THE METAL WELLNESS TOOLKIT

Perhaps the most practical step I took was creating a comprehensive wellness toolkit that provides concrete resources during challenging periods. Mine includes contact information for my healthcare providers and key support people, my list of early warning signs and corresponding action steps, techniques that have helped during past difficulties, resources for immediate support (crisis lines, online forums, my support group schedule), and meaningful reminders of my reasons for maintaining recovery, including a photo of my family and a brief letter to myself that I wrote during a particularly good period.

I keep both digital and physical versions of this toolkit—a folder on my phone and a small notebook in my desk drawer. During difficult times, when overthinking threatens to overwhelm me, having these resources readily available reduces the mental load of figuring out what to do or whom to contact.

This toolkit serves not only as a practical resource during difficult times but also as a tangible reminder of my commitment to ongoing wellness and the progress I've already made. On days when the noise in my head tries to convince me I haven't really made progress, this concrete evidence helps counter those thoughts.

Becoming the hero of your own story doesn't mean achieving perfect mental health or never struggling again. It means recognizing that you have both the right and the responsibility to play an active role in your ongoing care. It means building the knowledge, relationships, and tools that support your continued wellness. And perhaps most importantly, it means quieting the overthinking that keeps you stuck in passive patterns of responding to mental health challenges.

The noise may never completely disappear, but it loses much of its power when you stop being a passive character in your story and instead the protagonist actively shaping your journey toward continued wellness.

The noise may never completely disappear, but it loses much of its power when you stop being a passive character in your story. Instead, the protagonist actively shapes your journey toward continued wellness.

Conclusion

When I began writing this book, I sat at my desk and closed my eyes, trying to recall the exact moment when I first noticed the noise in my head had quieted. There wasn't a single dramatic instance, no cinematic epiphany where the overthinking suddenly stopped. Instead, there were countless small moments that gradually accumulated: the morning I watched the sunrise without analyzing my career path; the conversation with my kids where I remained fully present instead of mentally rehearsing work presentations; the night I fell asleep without reviewing every interaction from the day.

Recovery from the overthinking trap happens this way—not in one transformative moment, but in thousands of small victories where the space between your thoughts grows just a little wider, where the volume of the mental noise turns down just a notch, and where your capacity to be present expands by degrees.

Throughout these pages, we've explored the many faces of overthinking—how it manifests as rumination about the past, worry about the future, analysis paralysis, catastrophizing, and comparison thinking. We've examined how these patterns trap us in cycles that drain our energy, distance us from others, and diminish our experience of life. We've confronted the particular challenges men face in breaking these patterns, given cultural expectations around strength, self-reliance, and emotional control.

But more importantly, we've walked through practical approaches for quieting this mental noise: grounding techniques that bring you back to the present moment; cognitive strategies that help you recognize and challenge unhelpful thought patterns; mindfulness practices that create space between you and your thoughts; relationship skills that replace isolation with genuine connection; value clarification that guides you toward what truly matters; and sustainable self-care that builds resilience against future challenges.

My hope is that you've found strategies that resonate with your particular experience of overthinking. Not every approach works for everyone; what quiets the noise in my head might not work for yours. The journey toward mental peace is uniquely personal, requiring patience, self-compassion, and a willingness to experiment until you find your path forward.

Remember that this journey isn't about achieving perfect mental silence. Even after years of practice, my mind still generates unhelpful thoughts. The difference now is that I don't identify with them so completely, don't believe them so automatically, and don't allow them to dictate my actions and emotions as they once did. When the thoughts arise, I acknowledge them with awareness, and increasingly often, I can let them pass without being pulled into their current.

This is a practice, not a destination, something we work at daily rather than achieve once and for all. There will be setbacks along the way. The noise will sometimes return, especially during periods of stress, transition, or challenge. What matters isn't that we eliminate all difficult thoughts but that we develop the capacity to respond to them skillfully rather than react to them habitually.

For many of us, especially those who have experienced depression, anxiety, or significant life crises, there can be a lingering fear that the noise will return with its former intensity. I want to acknowledge that fear while also offering the perspective that comes from both personal experience and witnessing others' journeys: Each time you practice quieting the overthinking, you strengthen neural pathways that make future peace more accessible. You're not just managing today's mental noise; you're gradually rewiring your brain's default patterns.

While the tools and practices in this book are coping mechanisms to get through difficult periods, they're also investments in a fundamentally different relationship with your thoughts, one where you are the observer of your mental activity rather than its captive, where you can use thinking as a tool rather than being used by it, and where you can choose when to analyze and when to simply experience.

As you continue forward, I encourage you to be patient with yourself. Change happens gradually, often imperceptibly at first. Notice and celebrate the small victories: the moment you catch yourself ruminating and choose to redirect your attention; the time you resist the urge to mentally rehearse a conversation for the twentieth time; the evening you put down your phone instead of comparing your life to carefully curated social media presentations.

I also encourage you to share what you're learning. One of the most powerful ways to solidify new patterns is to articulate them to others. This doesn't mean you need to publicly discuss your most private struggles, but perhaps there's someone in your life who might benefit from hearing about a technique that's helped you, or maybe you notice a friend trapped in anxiety, and you can gently offer perspective.

The road from internal noise to mental peace ripples outward. As you learn to quiet the noise in your head, you become more present with those you love. As you develop self-compassion, you naturally extend more compassion to others. As you reconnect with what truly matters to you, you bring more authentic engagement to every area of your life.

The noise might never completely disappear, but it can become the background hum rather than the dominant soundtrack of your life. In that quieter mental space, something remarkable happens: You rediscover your capacity for joy, connection, creativity, and purpose. You reclaim not just your peace of mind, but your very life.

That reclamation, that return to yourself, is what this journey is ultimately about. And it begins anew each time you notice the noise and gently, persistently, choose a different way.

References

Aguilera, A., Villanueva-Moya, L. & Expósito, F. (2024). Mapping gender role stress scales utilities: A scoping review approach. *Frontiers in Psychology, 15*. https://doi.org/10.3389/fpsyg.2024.1436337

Al-Qahtani, A. M., Shaikh, M. A. K. & Shaikh, I. A. (2018). Exercise as a treatment modality for depression: A narrative review. *Alexandria Journal of Medicine, 54*(4), 429–435. https://doi.org/10.1016/j.ajme.2018.05.004

Appleton, J. (2018). The gut-brain axis: Influence of microbiota on mood and mental health. *Integrative Medicine: A Clinician's Journal, 17*(4), 28. https://pmc.ncbi.nlm.nih.gov/articles/PMC6469458/

Brown, A. (2025, May 2). *How therapy helps men with their mental health - the path to emotional healing*. Emerge Psychology Group. https://emergepg.com/blog/how-therapy-helps-men-with-their-mental-health-the-path-to-emotional-healing

Centers for Disease Control and Prevention. (2025, March 26). *Suicide data and statistics*. https://www.cdc.gov/suicide/facts/data.html

Churchill, W. S. (n.d.). *A quote by Winston S. Churchill*. Goodreads. https://www.goodreads.com/quotes/3270-success-is-not-final-failure-is-not-fatal-it-is

David, S. (2023, November 9). *Cognitive narrowing at work*. Linkedin. https://www.linkedin.com/posts/susanadavidphd_in-this-video-im-speaking-to-cognitive-narrowing-activity-7128451246557941760-P93J/

Donovan, M., Mackey, C. S., Platt, G. N., Rounds, J., Brown, A. N., Trickey, D. J., Liu, Y., Jones, K. M., & Wang, Z. (2020). Social isolation alters behavior, the gut-immune-brain axis, and neurochemical circuits in male and female prairie voles. *Neurobiology of Stress, 13*(100278), 100278. https://doi.org/10.1016/j.ynstr.2020.100278

Frankl, V. E. (2006). *Man's search for meaning*. Beacon Press. (Original work published 1946)

Frankl, V. E. (2018). *Man's Search For Ultimate Meaning*. Basic Books.

Friedman, B. (2019, June 27). *Male and depressed? Here's how recovery is possible.* FHE Health. https://fherehab.com/learning/male-and-depressed-recovery/

Fulmali, S., Shetty, P., Mane, A. & Uchit, G. (2018). Understanding masked depression: A clinical scenario. *Indian Journal of Psychiatry*, *60*(1), 97. https://doi.org/10.4103/psychiatry.indianjpsychiatry_272_17

Grosso, G., Galvano, F., Marventano, S., Malaguarnera, M., Bucolo, C., Drago, F. & Caraci, F. (2014). Omega-3 fatty acids and depression: Scientific evidence and biological mechanisms. *Oxidative Medicine and Cellular Longevity*, *2014*(1), 1–16. https://doi.org/10.1155/2014/313570

Howard, J. (n.d.). *A quote by Jane Howard*. Goodreads. https://www.goodreads.com/quotes/58361-call-it-a-clan-call-it-a-network-call-it

Jung, C. (n.d.). *A quote by C.G. Jung*. Goodreads. https://www.goodreads.com/quotes/441127-the-most-terrifying-thing-is-to-accept-oneself-completely

Kim, I.-B., Lee, J.-H. & Park, S.-C. (2022). The relationship between stress, inflammation, and depression. *Biomedicines*, *10*(8), 1929. https://doi.org/10.3390/biomedicines10081929

McKenzie, S., Collings, S., Jenkin, G. & River, J. (2018). Masculinity, social connectedness, and mental health: Men's diverse patterns of practice. *American Journal of Men's Health*, *12*(5), 1247–1261. Pubmed Central. https://doi.org/10.1177/1557988318772732

Najafi, K., Khoshab, H., Rahimi, N. & Jahanara, A. (2022). Relationship between spiritual health with stress, anxiety and depression in patients with chronic diseases. *International Journal of Africa Nursing Sciences*, *17*, 100463. https://doi.org/10.1016/j.ijans.2022.100463

Nickerson, C. (2023, October 23). *What is role strain? Definition and examples.* Simply Psychology. https://www.simplypsychology.org/what-is-role-strain-in-sociology.html

Nietzsche, F. (n.d.-a). *A quote by Friedrich Nietzsche*. Goodreads. https://www.goodreads.com/quotes/206149-amor-fati-love-your-fate-which-is-in-fact

Nietzsche, F. (n.d.-b). *A quote from The Invisible Leader*. Goodreads.com. Retrieved June 10, 2025, from https://www.goodreads.com/quotes/9084405-he-who-has-a-why-to-live-can-bear-almost

Noetel, M., Sanders, T., Gallardo-Gómez, D., Taylor, P., Cruz, B. del P., Hoek, D. van den, Smith, J. J., Mahoney, J., Spathis, J., Moresi, M., Pagano, R., Pagano, L., Vasconcellos, R., Arnott, H., Varley, B., Parker, P., Biddle, S. & Lonsdale, C. (2024). Effect of exercise for depression: Systematic review and network meta-analysis of randomised controlled trials. *The BMJ*, *384*(8417), e075847. https://doi.org/10.1136/bmj-2023-075847

Powell, A. (2018, April 9). *Harvard researchers study how mindfulness may change the brain in depressed patients*. Harvard University. https://news.harvard.edu/gazette/story/2018/04/harvard-researchers-study-how-mindfulness-may-change-the-brain-in-depressed-patients

Ramirez, J. L. & Badger, T. A. (2013). Men navigating inward and outward through depression. *Archives of Psychiatric Nursing, 28*(1), 21–28. https://doi.org/10.1016/j.apnu.2013.10.001

Rohn, J. (n.d.). *A quote by Jim Rohn*. Goodreads. https://www.goodreads.com/quotes/9042090-take-care-of-your-body-it-s-the-only-place-you

Rumi. (n.d.). *A quote by Rumi*. Goodreads. https://www.goodreads.com/quotes/103315-the-wound-is-the-place-where-the-light-enters-you

Sleiman, S. F., Henry, J., Al-Haddad, R., El Hayek, L., Abou Haidar, E., Stringer, T., Ulja, D., Karuppagounder, S. S., Holson, E. B., Ratan, R. R., Ninan, I., & Chao, M. V. (2016). Exercise promotes the expression of brain derived neurotrophic factor (BDNF) through the action of the ketone body β-hydroxybutyrate. *ELife, 5*(e15092). https://doi.org/10.7554/elife.15092

Socrates. (n.d.). *The secret of change (don't listen to Socrates)*. Enclaria: Influence Change at Work. https://www.enclaria.com/2018/10/25/the-secret-of-change-dont-listen-to-socrates/

Trachtenberg, E. (2024). The beneficial effects of social support and prosocial behavior on immunity and health: A psychoneuroimmunology perspective. *Brain, Behavior, & Immunity - Health*, 100758–100758. https://doi.org/10.1016/j.bbih.2024.100758

Tse, D. C. K. (2018). Volunteers' felt respect and its associations with volunteering retention, daily affect, well-being, and mortality. *The Journals of Gerontology: Series B, 75*(8). https://doi.org/10.1093/geronb/gby117

Vanninen, M. (2022, June 16). *How to silence your inner critic with courage*. Linkedin. https://www.linkedin.com/pulse/how-silence-your-inner-critic-courage-milja-vanninen

Wang, Y., Lippke, S., Miao, M. & Gan, Y. (2019). Restoring meaning in life by meaning-focused coping: The role of self-distancing. *PsyCh Journal, 8*(3), 386–396. https://doi.org/10.1002/pchj.296

Weininger, R. B. (2022, June 30). *Facing an existential vacuum today*. Psychology Today. https://www.psychologytoday.com/us/blog/heart-medicine-changing-world/202206/facing-existential-vacuum-today

Whittle, E. L., Fogarty, A. S., Tugendrajch, S., Player, M. J., Christensen, H., Wilhelm, K., Hadzi-Pavlovic, D. & Proudfoot, J. (2015). Men, depression, and coping: Are we on the right path? *Psychology of Men & Masculinity, 16*(4), 426–438. https://doi.org/10.1037/a0039024

Wooll, M. (2021, November 17). *You know you need human connection. Here's how to achieve it*. BetterUp. https://www.betterup.com/blog/human-connection

Zhang, M., Zhang, Y. & Kong, Y. (2020). Interaction between social pain and physical pain. *Brain Science Advances, 5*(4), 265–273. https://doi.org/10.26599/bsa.2019.9050023